INNER
CALM

INNER
CALM

A path to inner peace

MANUEL TRIGUERO

First edition: January 2022
Title: INNER CALM
Cover image: Dorothe
Copyright © 2022 Manuel Triguero
ISBN: 978-84-09-51774-9

To those who seek inner peace,
through silence and calm.

Index

Introduction

When your mind is calm there is no intention, no purpose in you. Your intellect rests; it does not seek any reason, it does not try to understand or to know anything; it does not seek understanding, nor any other form of thought. There is only a harmony, a union full of consonance with a hidden, hidden silence, which leads you to an immobile stillness, far from any disturbance, from any movement that could disturb that secret serenity in which you find an inner peace that reconciles you with "what you are", in the deepest part of yourself.

When you reach this link, it is as if you find a consonance, a cohesion with something deeper in you - that has always been there-, which leads you to establish a union with yourself, through a harmony that seeks balance and a calmness that dissolves the noise: all that mental clatter that floods the consciousness through thought, through all those images that you perceive in your own interior and that often cloud your reason, confusing your judgments and even your own understanding.

In the stillness the thought is tamed, the mind is pacified, which quiets down, submerging you little by little in a mysterious emptiness of silence and silence.

You feel the order, that everything has a more proportionate rhythm, more leisurely, which leads you to an affinity with all those things that surround you; to establish a much deeper bond with yourself and to identify yourself with "what you really are".

Only in such a state can this union exist, because you are no longer governed by the intention of your mind, by all those purposeless ideas that often cloud your reason and make you imagine reality in a wrong way.

Feeling the stillness makes you observe the emptiness, that uninhabited place inside you, freed from the bonds of the mind, where you find inner peace through silence.

It helps you to separate all those thoughts that at a given moment may become toxic. The fact of establishing a pause in time, allows you to make this choice, being able to focus only on those contents that keep a certain consonance with what you understand that you really are, with what is your "true purpose".

Thanks to the calmness you are present -you stop being asleep-, your body relaxes and the stillness penetrates you, in such a way that it eliminates all the barriers that separate you from that space where your "true self" is.

It is as if you were passing from darkness to light; as if you were leaving the surface where you usually move and moving to a much deeper dimension, which is that center where everything is created; a much more real world, where you just limit yourself to "be a witness", without anything conditioning you, and to be in contact with the truth, observing the present as it is, without resorting to the imagination or to the millions

of problems that are stored in your memory, waiting to
emerge in your consciousness.

1. Inner calm

Inner calm is a delicate state of mind, since it is something intangible, so imaginary that we only realize it exists when we feel its effects, when we perceive that trace that reminds us that we are in a state of silence that produces a stillness that suspends any sound, any outburst of noise that separates us from that stealth, from that mysterious secret that is our inner peace: that harmony that we appreciate when calm floods everything, when rest leads us to a placidity without thought, to an observation without ideas, without concepts, without judgments.

It is that peace that we feel in those moments of non-agitation in which we reach an inner stillness that leads us to a harmony in the deepest part of ourselves.

To be calm is to live in sanity, to be directed through prudence, to observe things from moderation, from caution, always leaving a pause to reflect, to pay attention in more detail and to notice other possible suggestions that are hidden behind all that you observe and that you have before you.

It is a state that leads you to recollection, to contemplate everything in a separate way, isolating the parts: all those elements that make up the reality of what you see, and that most of the time remain hidden, without being able to distinguish them, making you unable to discover the truth.

To become calm is not to numb the thought, but to temper the mind: all that turmoil of images that circulate through our consciousness in an impulsive way, without any kind of order.

It means to appease the noise that comes from the unconscious, from all those contents accumulated over time that try to emerge without any control, to take control of your own life; of what you have to think and what you must do, with hardly any time for you to deviate, to be able to decide for yourself.

It is a situation in which we simply let ourselves be carried away by silence, and accept that it is the stillness itself that guides us.

Without having the need to focus on a certain thought, we remain there, present, witnessing what happens within ourselves; without the obligation of having to judge anything; without taking care of labeling things, each mental content that we observe; these are moments in which we do not think about the past or the future.

It is as if we lose track of time; as if we were far away from all suffering, from all those thoughts that cause us pain and from those toxic emotions that often take hold of us.

To live in calm is to be in contact with yourself, with your own body; close to a center that is far from everything that can influence you from the outside, from that which can disturb an order that is only found there, in that world far from any tension that can only be accessed through relaxation and stillness.

Your body acquires a state of tranquility that spreads inside you, little by little, through a silence that envelops you and distances you from time and from everything that can influence you from the outside.

Calmness is a balm that makes you be above the pitfalls of thought; that leads you to the beginning - where everything originates-, far from the visible world where stimuli abound and you barely have time to appreciate anything, because sometimes these are quickly extinguished giving way to the next ones, clouding your vision of reality. A reality that you observe outside and that sometimes differs from the one that extends inside: the one that spreads through your mind through your own imagination, in a perpetual connection of images that bloom inside you endlessly.

HOW IT IS ACHIEVED

Inner calm is achieved when we connect with our "true self", which is found deep within ourselves, in a space of consciousness away from mental noise, where there is only silence, where there is an emptiness that can only be accessed from stillness, in a disposition of inner peace.

This is achieved when we manage to unite the outer silence with that deep peace that we can achieve if we move away from mental noise: from any psychic content that tries to steal our attention and keep us away from that union with "what we are"; which only occurs at a deeper level, within our inner world.

For this it is essential, first of all, to distance ourselves from everything that disturbs us, that disturbs our mind, creating a confusion that overwhelms us and makes us fall into carelessness, into a distraction that dazes us, leading us to drift, to the loss of attention on what really matters.

Pausing

To achieve calmness you should not force anything; just let some time pass so that your mind slowly pauses and all those automatic thoughts that invade us continuously stop appearing.

After that moment you begin to feel that you are in control, that you can direct the content that is in your consciousness.

Actually, in those moments, you are also using your mind, but in this case you are doing it in a voluntary, conscious way.

When there is no such pause and you do not observe what is happening within it, you simply let yourself be carried away by any thought that may arise at any given moment.

They are two different forms of mental functioning: one is totally unconscious, automatic, and acts in an autonomous way, without any control on your part; and the other is conscious, voluntary, because you are the one who controls everything that arises in your consciousness.

To reach calmness it is enough just not to think about anything, but in most cases this is not so easy: we are mentally active by nature, so we can hardly make a long pause to stop this way of functioning. Therefore, you need some time, it does not come quickly.

You can take control by establishing a pause when you want to reach it. Then you have to relax and begin to observe yourself internally making everything slow down. You will feel that your thoughts begin to slow down, which gives you time to stop and observe them, so that you have the opportunity to see how they pass, how they arise and soon fade away.

Little by little you begin to feel that you enter a different state, as if you were entering another much deeper dimension where everything seems to go slower.

In reality, it is about pausing and observing everything that happens in your consciousness, without focusing on anything in particular. In this way you can transcend everything that happens in your mind. It is the only way to be at that point where you can observe everything you think at a given moment.

Thanks to this pause we can establish, if we practice it frequently, a separation of that compulsive mental state in which we are immersed daily without being aware of it, which leads us to the realization of behaviors and habits that are conditioning our destiny, as they are nothing more than repetitive actions that are shaping us, that are directing us in many occasions by paths that we do not want.

Only from a state of stillness we can become aware of all these consequences, because we have enough space and time to observe ourselves, which leads us to know our inner workings and also the way we have to behave on the outside; through our behaviors, in our relationships with others, with those who surround us regularly.

If we manage to put it into practice at specific times, periodically, that alone will be enough to discover all the advantages of achieving this necessary pause in our mind, to be increasingly aware that we have a useful tool to control, in those moments when we need it, all that maelstrom of mechanical and automatic thoughts that flood us, and that when they are toxic cause us suffering and divert us from our true path; they force us not to be us, because they separate us from what we really are, from our "true essence", forcing us to perform a series of habits acquired through repetition with which we are not really happy, since they lead us to perform a series of actions contrary to what we really want to do, to lead a coherent life that has to do with what we want to be in the depths of ourselves.

You can make everything stop for a few moments, reach the suspension of all the actions you are doing. In those moments a function is activated in your mind that calms the movement, so that even the thought itself passes at a different speed, so that you have a space to examine all that circulates in your consciousness.

And all because of that stop, that pause, where for a few seconds you put your mind in standby mode, as in an intermission, setting a distance between each thought, which allows you to establish a break to resolve, in a more appropriate way, everything that in those moments is integrated in your consciousness, which in most cases you fail to grasp because of the vividness of all those contents that move incessantly inside your mind.

The most frequent thing is that we let ourselves be guided by everything that comes to our consciousness, since it is what we are accustomed to. We are not trained to face all that whirlwind of automatic contents that come from our unconscious and that flood us without us being able to stop them at first.

However, if within all that whirlwind of automatic thoughts we manage to establish a pause, we will be able to stop that repetitive process that leads us to perform automatic behaviors, in the form of unwanted habits, which lead us to perform a series of activities in which we can easily waste time and spend a huge amount of energy without any apparent reward.

Knowing how to make that pause leads to knowing oneself better, to understanding the meaning of hidden things and to finding the truth of what surrounds us; and to discovering a "clarity" that is only accessible from one's own consciousness, far from the noise of the mind and all those distractions of the external world that confuse us and lead us down unwanted paths.

To reach this pause, through which you can even gain control of your own thoughts, requires a previous practice in which you learn to find spaces of silence that you can create in the daily chores of your daily life.

Being aware

You can only control this situation if you are aware that this can happen, to the extent that you become aware of it; in this way you can take control of this process and continue to maintain yourself in that state of inner peace in which you are alone with yourself and you become the observer of everything that happens within you; at the same time that you take control of each thought that slowly arises in your consciousness.

In those moments it is enough to let yourself go. If a thought arises suddenly, it is enough to let it pass; in this way you will remain in that state and nothing will take you out of it.

Images, ideas, memories may also arise involuntarily, but you will be aware of all these elements and you will have enough time to stop and look at them, as if they were appearing on a screen and you were observing them from a distance, from a distance; as if they had nothing to do with you.

In those moments your posture is that of an observer who simply limits himself to perceiving what passes in front of him, without the obligation of having to judge anything, of having to put a label on every object that arises.

If you stay in this position, you will observe that the frequency of appearance of each thought or image decreases, that the time in which there is only silence or an empty space that is not occupied by any content, by any memory, becomes longer and longer.

There will be times when you feel that there is a resistance to stay there, since your mind, by its very nature, will always tend to be active, to spend energy through the repetitive creation of images. This is why sometimes you will feel the need to get out of that state of inner peace and return to normal activity, which is carried out through a repetitive chain of thoughts and actions.

With practice you can become aware that this can happen, so you will gradually find it easier to extend that calm situation for a longer period of time. By being aware of the mechanisms that your mind uses to bring you back to the normal state, you can not let y-ourself go and stay longer in that position of stillness.

Through relaxation

You cannot relax your mind if you keep yourself in tension. If for some reason you are watching a stimulus or something worries you, you keep your focus of attention there without being able to separate yourself from it.

To stop somehow all that frenetic and constant activity that exists in your mind it is necessary that you enter a state of relaxation.

You must first start with the body, by observing its functioning, focusing on your breathing, feeling how you introduce air into your lungs and at the same time expelling it. In this simple way your mental activity slows down, thoughts cease to circulate in your consciousness and thus opens an open space where peace reigns and envelops you.

Not forcing anything

It is about looking for those moments of stillness, but without forcing anything. Everything should be natural, it should arise in a simple, easy way, without too much pressure to reach that situation.

We should not feel obliged, so to speak, to find that position that puts us in contact with a deeper level that exists within ourselves and that is far from the noise of the mind and the repetitive and automatic thoughts that constantly arise in our consciousness and encompass everything, forcing us to put the focus of attention on a certain content, without us hardly realizing it, that this is happening within us.

To reach that state you must allow your inner peace to gradually take over that inner space, where you can observe yourself away from any distractions. You can only achieve this if you do it naturally, freeing yourself from any tension that you may have at that moment because of any worry that is going around in your mind at that moment.

When you can best connect with your inner space is when you do not force anything, when you let silence alone take you to that place. It is not about making a specific effort to reach that state of stillness, it is simply about letting yourself be swept away by the calmness itself.

At the moment you try to force that situation, you are still aware of what is happening in your mind, you are still using it to try to create or reach that condition of inner peace. In this way it will be much more difficult for you to reach that point.

You must let go of everything that prevents you from reaching that phase of stillness, until you manage to enter it. Once you get everything is somewhat easier, you just have to limit yourself to observe your consciousness from the calm.

You do not feel the need to force anything, since in those cases there is no intention in you, no interest to perform an upcoming action; you are just limiting yourself to be present to that emptiness that gradually expands, as your own mental activity becomes slower.

BENEFITS

Only when we act from calmness, from that peaceful raft of oil that is peace without fissures, from that place where there is balance and moderation, we can act in consonance, from a wisdom that leads you to reason always from moderation, through a mature logic, from a cautious reflection.

Only when we are calm are we prudent, we act with tact. Our judgments seem to be more mature, as if we see everything from another dimension, from a distance, with measured temperance and prudent reflection.

If we learn to observe everything from stillness, we will obtain a serenity that will help us in the most complicated moments, in those most compromising situations in which we lose the sense of ourselves and we let ourselves be dragged by anguish and anxiety unconsciously.

It enables you another way of being in the world, another way of seeing things more serene, more imperturbable; as if you establish a distance between everything that happens and yourself.

Knowing how to stop in time leads you to have a greater understanding, because you have a space to find a logic, a reason for what you have before you at every moment: whether it is a person, a fact or a thought that has arisen in your consciousness and you have to decide whether to follow it or not.

You have enough time to pay attention to what flows in your mind, to pay attention to what you think, and to notice the details of each judgment you make, of the deductions you create to try to explain those things you still do not understand, although you perceive them daily.

You can distinguish each idea, that which is only your own imagination, and all those sensations that come along with each image, with each thought that emerges and leads you to design approaches and beliefs, by which you conceive opinions that create the conviction that the world is only as you expect it to be, without having the slightest suspicion that it could be otherwise.

In those small intervals where you move to another dimension, much slower, you find yourself with the capacity to be able to consciously put aside, that which is not useful to you, because it has no attraction for you or simply because you do not find any benefit in it. You can appreciate, with greater clarity, that which is not favorable to you, in view of the objectives you have set: the path you intend to follow.

It leads you to find yourself

Through stillness you can establish a postponement, an interval to ensure that you will always remain the same, despite what you find around you and the anguish you feel when you cease to be: when you lose control of your own being.

When you take control you become what you really are, you recover your true identity, which has nothing to do with that image created in your mind. You get to know yourself, far from all those labels you have unconsciously put on yourself.

And you begin to walk a different inner path, away from the obstacles of thought. You begin to see things from another perspective, from your own inner world, where you have the ability to distance yourself from all those illusory beliefs that you have developed within you and that have led you to imagine an unreal world, on many occasions.

Inner calm allows you to grow inside, to transform yourself if necessary, distancing yourself from the deception of the mind, from all that frenetic activity that leads you to be permanently active, accumulating a tension that sometimes takes you to the limit of your own strength.

From stillness it is easier to know yourself and who you are. When you discover this, you no longer let yourself be dominated by your mind, you begin to act in a more conscious way, gaining control of your inner world.

You can thus create an existence much more coherent and adapted to who you are: closer to the truth, because everything you decide will come from an integrity determined by what you really think, away from any external influence and psychic noise, which usually takes hold of us and leads us down unwanted paths.

It will help you to continue on the right path, to not stop and to be a witness of everything that happens while you follow that path that begins in you and that you need to follow in order to feel yourself in everything you do.

Calmness leads you to act accordingly, having a congruence with what you are, with what you really want to do in every moment.

If you find yourself in a situation of calm and silence, it will be much easier for you to have access to that other dimension that lies deep within yourself.

Inner calm is a source of understanding that helps you to contemplate things through a process where you do not judge or label anything, where you just live in the moment, to look at everything from within yourself, where all changes occur and fears are resolved.

When we are calm we are mere observers of what is happening, both outside and inside ourselves. We do not feel the need to force things; to act impulsively, allowing ourselves to be carried away by our thoughts.

When we find calm, we feel at peace with ourselves. In those moments there is nothing to divert us from that center that we only find when we reach that point where we become observers, where we establish a distance between us and what happens in our own mind.

Calmness allows you to observe your inner self from a higher, singular location; from which you can distinguish everything: to glimpse what is good in you, what springs up in your conscience and what leads you to be and behave in a certain way, to think always in a certain way.

It makes you penetrate, in a deeper way, into what you do not understand, what you still cannot discern because of the lack of awareness to which you are usually subjected because you live in an irrational and unconscious world, dominated by automatic processes that you yourself create within the context in which you live.

Calmness is the path that allows you to be an exceptional spectator of everything that happens. It enables you to contemplate everything from a privileged position, away from the influence of the mind and external distractions, which often take over and lead you to a disorderly action: to lose control and let yourself be carried away by the first thing you think.

Thanks to it you can contemplate what in a normal situation goes unnoticed, because it hardly gives you time to attend to all that content that crowds in your mind, that comes from the unconscious in an impulsive and mechanical way and that often traps you in a perpetual loop of repetitive thoughts.

In a normal situation it is possible that we let ourselves be dragged by the first thing we think, because we do not have this space to establish this necessary pause that leads us to observe everything from a stillness that positions us in a privileged place, from which we can observe everything in a more leisurely, more objective way; where we have the opportunity to contemplate the facts from another point of view closer to the truth, closer to the reality of what is happening.

It is a situation in which all the mental noise coming from repetitive thoughts ceases, it is as if we were situated at another level of consciousness from which we can observe everything that happens and at the same time we find the facility to let pass each content that is occupying our mind: all those images that are emerging from the bottom of our memory and that are passing through our consciousness in an incessant and repetitive way.

It is advisable to make this stop frequently, because in some way it leads you to an encounter with yourself and, from the place where this occurs, you are no longer affected by all those influences that come from outside and those other contents that also arise in your own mind, because you place yourself in a place where you can observe in an objective way all that is happening, both outside and inside yourself; you can only achieve this if you access this space of consciousness, away from the usual noise of the mind.

If you get used to find it frequently, you will notice its benefits, especially in your way of being in the world. You will have a different attitude towards difficulties, because you will get used to observe things from another perspective, much more distant and objective than usual.

Thanks to the calm you will have another vision of reality, with less interference, more liberated from all those elements that often prevent us from seeing what surrounds us with sufficient clarity.

Once you get into that place, you stay away from thoughts, and if they try to occupy that space of consciousness, you can observe them from a position that allows you to establish a distance between those contents -which can arise to consciousness- and yourself.

You simply become a mere observer of everything that happens within you, and you limit yourself to listening to yourself through a language that you are able to understand, because it is so clear that you come to understand everything that was previously unexplained.

Conscious calm leads you to look without thinking too much; it makes you examine everything you observe without having to weigh anything, without the need to judge, which always exists when we value everything that happens, when we appreciate everything that happens and then try to qualify it to give it a name, to classify it in our memory.

It leads you to unblocking, to freeing yourself and to entering a wider space that allows you to observe things from another dimension; to grasp the full magnitude of reality; to calibrate things in their right measure, reaching a balance that is only reached when you feel that there is a consonance and a union with yourself.

We have another perception of reality

Thanks to the calm we can get to have another perception of reality; acquire a much more objective and less contaminated vision, because we will observe everything from within ourselves, outside the influences of visible distractions: Of the stimuli from the outside, which often lead us to have a wrong vision of reality, because we feel confused by the amount of content that constantly comes to us from outside and that we find it difficult to assimilate, because we barely have time to organize all that information that often overwhelms us and makes our own reason become clouded, when we are faced with too intense stimuli.

When we reach this state of inner peace, we observe things as they really are, our perception does not seem so contaminated, because there is a decrease in the amount of information that we capture in those moments; we remain alert, attentive, but without the need to focus on something specific, without the obligation of having to make an effort to attend to a certain content.

Such a state helps you to decipher in a more impartial way everything you perceive. It places you in a neutral, objective place, where your reason becomes sensible and your understanding more prudent. From there you guess everything with greater clarity: everything that afflicts you, your judgments and even your own feelings when you notice that there is something that affects you.

Calmness leads you to the light, to see everything with greater clarity, with greater precision; it is freed from chaos, from the confusion of thought, which with its anarchy often leads you to a disorder that makes you live in disorder, in a constant noise that agitates you inside and does not let you feel harmony: that chord rhythm that is your own peace at rest, that stillness that leads you to inner balance, sensible and stable.

You stop dreaming and begin to see things as they really are, without that desire to make assumptions and create fantasies that are only mere inventions of your own imagination, which needs to constantly invent to find an exit door, a reason to find a meaning to that which has none; a cause that makes you find the origin of that which you do not understand, that which you are not able to interpret because you have not yet experienced it.

Through this pause, which you can manage to establish through daily practice, you get a different perspective of the reality around you, because you have a tool that allows you to perceive things more clearly, with enough time to sort out all those little details that in most cases go unnoticed and are important to understand everything that happens to us, to reach an objective and reliable interpretation of everything that happens to us.

This leads us, in a way, to accept the facts as they are happening, without falling into too many interpretations; it gives us the wisdom to accept things as they are, because in those moments we are away from the mental noise and the influence of all those thoughts that often flood us, obscuring our reason, confusing us, making us divert our attention elsewhere.

Making that pause is always beneficial, because it allows you to clean your mind of toxic thoughts and contents that invade you daily, in your daily life, and force you to have a negative view of reality or of what is happening at every moment.

Disconnecting, even if it is only for a moment from everything that surrounds us, is always beneficial, since it allows you to have some time to sort out your ideas, which sometimes crowd one after another and accumulate in such a way that they make you feel confused, not knowing what to do really.

You will be able to observe the world with a different look, from a more objective point of view, closer to "what everything is".

In this way your mind clears, leaving a space to establish that necessary meeting with yourself that puts you in that position in which you begin to see things from another perspective, deeper and more authentic; that helps you somehow to not get carried away by the daily stress and anxiety that you may feel because of your lifestyle and all those circumstances that surround you, that make you behave in a mechanical and repetitive way, as if you were a robot programmed by yourself.

This is the best way to overcome uncertainty. If you limit yourself to observe what is inside you, you will come to understand without effort everything that is hidden from your understanding.

Only from a calm gaze can you realize that which is hidden and does not allow you to see reality as it is: that which envelops you in such a way that it leads you to a space of doubt that you do not know how to manage, so that in the end you cannot distinguish the true from the false; the real from the illusory.

Without knowing it, within us there are complex enigmas that drive us to change our minds and thoughts very quickly. They alter our own vision of things and become visible every time we encounter a difficulty in guessing reality.

From calmness you can contemplate everything that is hidden within you; everything that has an uncertain origin, that you do not know from where it arises, but that sometimes appears intensely as an impulse that causes you an agitation that leads you to restlessness.

Without calmness you cannot appreciate every instant, you cannot stop to observe carefully those objects that appear before you; or the sounds that may be around you; or those sensations that occur in your own interior.

With time, and by paying attention, we will be able to draw within ourselves an objective evaluation of each thing we see. But for this we must stay awake and have enough stillness to know and classify each content in its right measure, in a clear way.

It gives us more knowledge

Calmness provides us with more knowledge about everything around us and inside ourselves. Thanks to that pause that we establish when we look at something with the intention of knowing it, of reaching its total understanding, we obtain a greater control over all those elements that arise in our mind -at that precise moment- related to what we are trying to understand, to find out.

It helps us to have a greater understanding of all those things that we want to know, that we need to master in order to solve all those difficulties that arise in our daily life. He who knows how to find peace, in moments of difficulty, has a tool of the first order to solve his problems little by little, because he does not let himself be carried away by adversity, he does not allow an impediment, an obstacle, to take over his mind and subdue him.

We will learn to face the reality that surrounds us in a different way, with other much more powerful tools. We will acquire more knowledge from our experiences, because we will have the necessary time to make a much more complete reading of what is happening to us; getting to understand much better the circumstances that surround us.

We will develop better in the context in which our life takes place. Each experience will be richer and richer for us, because we will have the opportunity to draw a greater number of conclusions and information that will help us in the future, when we have to face similar situations. We will be able to reach a new way of being in the world, much slower, with a greater control over ourselves.

What will make you find all that great wealth that lies within you and that we do not always have the opportunity to discover to be only focused on what happens outside; trapped by all those stimuli and influences that are in the material world and that make us live constantly in a loop that often seems to have no end.

Only those who guide their steps from stillness, can more easily solve all those mysteries that surround us throughout our lives, and that are related to issues that have to do with existence, with what we are and what we could become if we manage to eliminate everything that prevents us from being ourselves; that represses and blocks us.

There will be things that will begin to make sense, because this situation will allow us to go into the causes of everything that happens.

It allows you to decide better

It enables you to reach that interval in which you can stop thinking and opt for the best possible alternative when choosing an act, or an outcome to all those ideas that crowd hastily in your consciousness and that often do not allow you to distinguish reality.

Our decisions will take another determination, because they will be taken with another will, they will start from a purpose adopted in a position of stillness, so they will be more stable and balanced; they will maintain a great firmness and their permanence will be greater in time.

Everything that we consider, from a situation of inner calm, will generate in us a greater confidence. To pause at the right moment generates in us a greater security, it helps us to believe that we are in control and that we act with the certainty of knowing that at that moment we are doing the right thing.

Acting in this way leads us to the conviction that we are more authentic, more true to ourselves, that our conclusions are closer to the truth; and that the decisions we make in those moments of reflection keep us away from error, from that confusion that takes hold of us when we drive ourselves wildly, without a direction that leads us to observe things in a slower way, to a calmer decision making, more in line with what we want deep down inside ourselves.

All this will be reflected in a much more moderate, gentler and kinder way of acting. Those around us will quickly appreciate it, they will pick up on your temperance: that moderation when you do things or when you communicate with them.

The fact of being able to make that pause makes it easier for you to choose what you think is best for you at any given moment. All this will bring as a consequence a greater success at the time of looking for solutions; at the time of taking the decisions that more suit us, according to the circumstances.

To take advantage of this pause can be advantageous to you, because you will always have a space to make the most convenient decision, the one that best suits what you really want to do.

It takes you away from any influence

Thanks to the feeling of stillness that we experience, we allow everything to happen without intervening too much. We just let it happen without forcing, so that nothing affects us. Unlike what happens in a normal situation, where we are aware of everything that affects us in such a way that it influences the way we behave, the way we think and our attitude in the face of difficulties.

It is as if we were far away from everything that could affect us, but at the same time taking into account all the details of what surrounds us, both outside and inside ourselves.

When we manage to reach that moment, there is nothing that disturbs us; either from outside or any thought that emanates from our consciousness with the idea of diverting us from our focus of attention, which in those moments is directed towards ourselves.

We will achieve that our mind moves less and less away from that center; that external distractions do not take hold of us, which continuously overwhelm us with stimuli that make us lose control and attention of what really matters: ourselves and what we really want.

Thanks to calmness you can keep your attention on a certain point that at that moment interests you for some reason. If we are not in that state of relaxation, it is easy for us to deviate from our focus of attention and our gaze is fixed on other stimuli that may be nearby; when you are in a state of relaxation you are aware of this and have more chances to avoid it.

Thanks to calmness you see the "clarity" in everything you think; it is like a window through which light enters your mind and extinguishes any shadow that has to do with past conflicts.

This stillness makes you escape from the noise of memories; it takes you away from all those mechanisms that exhaust your energy making you live in a superficial reality, where you barely have time to form your own reflections that lead you to discover the truth.

In the same way, you will also not be affected, in this situation, by the external influence, by the distractions that exist outside; you will also stay away from that possibility, as if there were nothing close to you that could distract you in those moments. This situation keeps you momentarily distanced from the outside, from everything that is around you.

It helps us to be more conscious

Calmness helps us to reach that state of consciousness where you can establish a separation between what you observe and yourself.

From inner peace you can become conscious more easily, because in such a situation nothing distracts you, there is nothing from outside that can lead you to another place; nor anything coming from your own mind either. Therefore, it is easy to become aware of what is happening in those moments inside you.

Thanks to the stillness that is achieved through that inner calm that is reached when you manage to disconnect from the manifest world, you can reach a state of consciousness that allows you to establish a distance between you and everything that may arise in your mind, coming from all those contents stored over time in the deepest part of your memory.

From inner calm you enter, therefore, into full consciousness, as long as this is accompanied by a true observant attitude, which has no intention of judging and labeling anything, which forces you just to be present, to be a witness of everything that happens.

In this way, nothing will be able to affect you, to influence you; at least during those brief periods in which you put this into practice.

With time, this new attitude will be transferred to your daily life. You will feel that same stillness, that same inner peace in every little action you do, in the chores of your daily life.

Thanks to this practice of becoming conscious, through stillness and silence, you will get into the habit of looking inside yourself more often, which will help you to discover a world unknown to you until then.

When you are aware, from the stillness, of everything that happens, your concern decreases and many things begin to change. You feel more and more present and your mind gradually frees itself from that constant mechanism that tries to condition it through automatic thoughts that are imprinted on the consciousness at high speed.

You feel in those moments that you begin to move away from the rush and all those influences that you find out there and that in most of the occasions trap you in such a way that you let yourself be carried away by them, without having the opportunity to exercise a control over yourself that prevents you from establishing a distance over those external stimuli that overwhelm you.

The mental noise, composed of all those automatic thoughts that arise from your unconscious, will gradually diminish, all those images that arise repeatedly in your consciousness and that cloud your vision and lead your attention to another more distant place will be reduced.

When you are conscious, from the calm, you stop living in discontent: in that permanent disillusionment that sometimes fills you with pessimism and leads you to boredom, to feel a great indifference for everything that happens in your immediate environment.

In a situation of stillness every moment will have a meaning for you; you will begin to exist in a different way, with much less limitations, being much more conscious and profound.

Thanks to the calmness we remain absent, away from what surrounds us and that in many occasions confuses us. It is a way to leave momentarily, while remaining in the same place, but in a much more conscious way.

It takes you to control

If you learn to open those parentheses, in the moments when they are necessary, you will always get to be in control in every situation; you will direct your life with greater audacity, because this way of proceeding will always guide you along the most appropriate path: the one that best suits who you really are.

It will lead you to always proceed from a harmony with yourself, because you will stop acting through those acquired habits that often have nothing to do with your true desires, with your "true purpose", with that ultimate goal that everyone has.

Thanks to this pause that we can establish, we get control over ourselves, so that we can influence our way of focusing our own thinking and also when it comes to redirect our behaviors, because this pause facilitates the decision we have to make before taking any action; it gives us a space where we can choose the best possible option, depending on each circumstance.

In these cases the actions we take will always be much more adapted to what we really want to do.

Inner calmness brings you in control of yourself; it allows you not to deviate from the route marked by your "true purpose": by what you should focus on in order to follow the path that best suits "what you really are".

Stillness allows you to not get carried away by all those impulses that arise from your own unconscious and that flood your mind forcing you to perform a series of often unwanted actions. By having control of what happens in your consciousness, you can somehow divert that uncontrolled energy that often takes over you and leads you to act like a robot, automatically and unconsciously.

You will acquire greater control over yourself, because you will no longer let yourself be governed by every situation in which you live. Everything in your environment, at every moment, will be secondary, because what is in your inner world will always have predilection; you will be guided by those thoughts that go in line with you, and not by any distraction coming from any object that is close to you.

Thanks to inner calm you will stop being a slave of everything that goes through your head; you will stop repeating over and over again the same thoughts. When you connect with yourself, your mind will stop being automatic and you will be responsible for everything that passes through your consciousness, without having to manipulate anything, you will let yourself be carried only by what you feel in that emptiness, because there is only a deep silence that leads you to be the owner of that domain.

It is then when you acquire control of all your reactions; of all your impulses, which are accustomed to arise at any moment from the depths of your unconscious and which hover over you constantly forcing you to exist in a world that makes you live like a robot, because they force you to always walk along mechanical paths and habits that you have acquired over time.

Thanks to inner calm you acquire a knowledge about yourself that can lead you to control everything you think at a given moment, as long as you are in a calm situation where stillness reigns and there is no noise, both external and internal, that can disturb you; it is the only way to find that inner peace that makes you keep a distance with everything that happens both outside and within your own interior.

It all starts with you. Transformation is only possible if you focus on the mastery you can exercise over yourself, over your own mind; through the exercise of observation of consciousness, from where you can delve into all those contents that arise from the depths of your memory.

It helps us to overcome difficulties

If we manage to reach this state of stillness frequently, we will have a tool of the first order to face any difficulty that comes our way and that we find difficult to solve through normal means.

Thanks to the calmness we are able to deepen in a more effective way in that which is unknown to us or involves a great difficulty; and thanks to this full attention that allows us to observe without distractions and focused on what really matters, we can solve many puzzles and difficulties that often arise in our daily lives, in the world around us.

In this way you will be able to check and take stock of everything that has happened to you up to that moment. You will be able to confront reality with the conclusions you have drawn from all the events you have experienced.

It can be an effective way to resolve pending conflicts and to overcome all those difficulties that have become a problem for you over time, turning into obstacles that hinder your development and your own personal well-being, because they prevent you from enjoying life, turning it into a permanent complication, full of hindrances and setbacks.

Through calmness you can achieve great advances that with time will be reflected in your way of being in the world and in the way you face each and every one of the difficulties that life puts in your way, through the different circumstances that you are going to live.

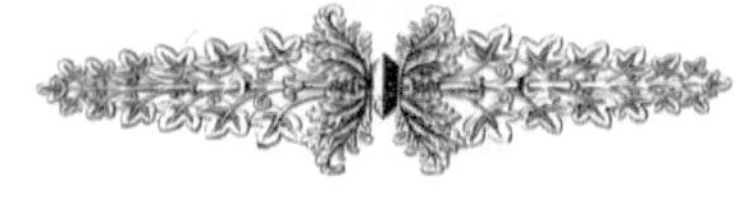

2. Silence

To reach calm also requires a regular contact with silence, which is a source of creativity because it helps you to focus on what you want in each moment, which helps you to discover the most valuable contents that exist within you.

Calm is easy to achieve if you manage to disconnect at some point every day, if you look for spaces of silence where nothing can distract you or take you to a different place.

Silence is nothing more than the key to enter that universe of calm and stillness where you really feel free of everything that usually occupies your mind, which always tries to make you end up doing something: an action or use your time in a specific activity, which is usually always the same.

Silence is a source of richness, since the best ideas that we can develop are born in principle from emptiness, they are not contaminated with any toxic element nor are they influenced by other external aspects that have nothing to do with it.

If you get used to using silence as a means to find inner calm, you will be aware of your own emotions; as well as of all the things you have imagined to try to escape from what you find difficult to understand.

We should not be afraid of silence; on the contrary, whenever possible we should seek it, access it; because it is the means, the door that allows us to enter into our own inner world, where we can experience a healing peace that allows us to reconcile with ourselves, to return to the path we should never have left; it puts us back on the path that deep within ourselves we know we must travel to live in harmony with "what we are".

How to reach it

It can be said that you have reached mental silence when no thought influences or affects you. It happens in those moments in which you limit yourself to observe without judging, without letting yourself be carried away by the energy flows that arise from your mind in the form of thoughts and images.

In such a situation, we become aware of all that, so we can get to control it if we practice it regularly and look for those moments in the day to get away from both physical and mental noise, establishing a distance between that which distracts us and ourselves.

When you are in silence it is not necessary to think about something in particular, you are not obliged to focus your attention on a particular subject. It is simply enough to let yourself be carried away by what comes to your mind, by what emerges from your memory and invades your consciousness, but in a distant way, without being affected, without being influenced by its content.

Thanks to silence you manage to stop all that maelstrom of images that crowd your consciousness and that in many occasions make you have moments of confusion, because you do not have enough time to organize all that accumulation of contents that arise in a disorganized and mechanical way; and that in many occasions leads us to such a mental confusion that affects our attention and produces a psychic imbalance that becomes difficult to control.

Silence provides us with a propitious ground to direct what exists within ourselves; all those impulses that flood us unconsciously and lead us to actions that we can hardly avoid, since we are used to act that way: following those bursts of energy that take hold of us and prevent us from conducting ourselves freely.

Everything that affects us, therefore, we will see it in a distant, distant way, separated from what we are, and therefore we will understand it as something that has nothing to do with us; as an aspect that belongs to another sphere that is not ours; as something that is composed of a series of contents that have come and have been created from the outside, that have been propitiated by other external forces. We have assimilated them because our perceptive system has captured them and we have internalized them in such a way that they have become part of our memory.

Everything that affects you or that produces a shadow in your mind fades away when you enter your inner world, through silence, and you stop acting like a robot and return to yourself.

Thanks to silence and observation we can separate all those contents -which do not belong to us- from what we are, thus achieving that we are not affected in the least by all those prejudices, false beliefs, toxic emotions and negative thoughts that we sometimes encounter.

The calm that is acquired, in this case, is the best medicine for all those conflicts that are created in your mind. Thanks to the stillness that you achieve in those moments of inner calm, you can put in order what is disordered, find the true meaning of what you have not yet come to understand.

It is the perfect tool to generate other kinds of thoughts that help you to see with much more clarity the reality that surrounds you, to find the truth.

Being conscious, through silence, eliminates all worries, because it distances you from any agitation, from all those things that alter your inner world causing anxiety and anguish.

It can help you to change, to transform yourself into another person with much less anger, farther away from affliction and anger, with much less setbacks.

If you go into that inner space, where there is only calm and you become fully conscious, you will come to observe the world with another attitude, and you will discover that through silence you can face all those problems that you have been finding in your life and that have been worrying you so much.

Only when you find yourself in that situation, you can verify the great benefits of silence; you will be aware of the reality in which you have lived until that moment: a reality lacking in understanding that has made you insist on a world where you have hardly been you, in most of the circumstances that have surrounded you.

INNER PEACE

Silence is our main ally, since through it we can enter into that world, which is not easy to access, where stillness reigns and is conducive to achieve inner peace: which is nothing more than a state in which you are alone with yourself and observe your mind without any distraction from it.

Inner peace is reached by attaining mental stillness, when you manage to stabilize and put at rest all that amalgam of constant thoughts that frequently flood you. Only in those moments, through this exercise of calmness, can you calm the agitation that is in you: all that mental turmoil that is constantly breaking your balance and does not allow you the necessary stability to think and act with moderation, with enough sense so that everything goes in consonance with yourself, with "what you really are".

If you want to find harmony within yourself, that quality that makes you always find the right proportion and balance of everything you think and feel, there must be a consonance, a unity brought about by that inner peace that is only reached when everything ceases, when you find a truce in which everything is interrupted; in which you yourself abandon yourself in a placid calm that appeases the impulses and all those outbursts caused by the urgency of the mind, by its desire to keep you always active, by its energetic yearning to push you always to action.

It is only acquired if you manage to reach that necessary tranquility through silence, knowing how to stop in time every impulse, every incitement coming from within yourself, and not letting yourself be carried away by noise, by every external influence or by any other influence that tries to divert you from that point where peace is found and everything is tamed, through a stealth that placates any distraction and all those unconscious acts that push us to leave that center, where we find ourselves.

You have time

When you achieve true "inner peace" you reach a process in which some functions of your mind cease; the activity becomes much slower and the urgency to move on to the next thought in a rush disappears. You can notice that there is no need to maintain that endless train of mental content that repeats itself over and over again, taking over all the space that is your consciousness.

You have time to manage and govern all those images that then become ideas that are reproduced automatically without you being able to have control over them under normal conditions.

You have a longer period of time, an interval, to perceive all those small details that often go unnoticed but are important to understand reality in an objective way; to appreciate in a more complete way the state of things, the facts that happen and the place where the truth is.

Thanks to those moments of peace brought about by silence, we can become people very different from what we are, since we will no longer be driven by our mind, but by what lies beyond, at another level that can only be accessed through stillness and observation without judgment.

You come to have another vision of yourself, because this way of being also influences your way of proceeding, your behaviors and the way you contemplate all that happens within yourself.

You will be able to distinguish your best attributes, all those skills that remain stored and do not emerge because you have never had the opportunity to look at them; going through life too fast, without looking at all that you carry inside to be able to bring it out when necessary.

Having this tool makes you see existence from another point of view, with another attitude, in a more integral way, free of those ties of the mind that often cover our reason with blurred judgments that lead us down confusing and uncertain paths.

Helps you resolve conflicts

When you live far from the predicament and the suffocation of haste, you are in a favorable position to face all those conflicts that hinder your life; you have a useful mechanism to get out of every quagmire, every setback that appears along the way.

It is a quite valid means to find the most appropriate remedy to each inconvenience, since in this way you can meditate observing many more alternatives; to reach better solutions, to reach, in this way, the best possible outcome to all those problems that little by little are burdening you with an uncomfortable suffering.

When the noise of your mind ceases, thoughts are suspended and you become part of a calm where you find that peace that on many occasions you have needed to face, in a precise way, all those conflicts that have complicated your existence; all those problems that have prevented you from seeing the clarity to get a precise answer, an appropriate way out.

It is a way to be more awake, because thanks to this state we notice more easily the origin of everything that happens, the components that cause the situations and many circumstances that surround us.

You observe everything more carefully

That inner peace that you feel in those moments, makes you become the observer of your own thoughts, of your own mind, of everything that happens in it, thus achieving a separation that allows you to preserve that state of stillness thanks to which you stay in that "center" that is your inner being, from which you can observe everything that happens within yourself, in your inner world; to the extent that allows you to keep that distance on any mental content or any emotion that you may feel.

All this cannot take place until you reach, through silence, that inner peace through which you manage to separate everything that is not yours -because it has come to you from outside- from what you really are, deep inside yourself.

In this way we reach an inner peace that allows us to observe everything more closely, to suspend ourselves in a secret rest where we can contemplate every mystery: all those doubts that we carry hidden inside ourselves.

It is the best way to reach an inner peace that in most cases is not possible due to the daily hustle and bustle that floods us and that takes us away from that center where we find ourselves, within our own interior, in those spaces of silence and stillness in which we can observe with clarity every thought and every image that circulates in our consciousness; whether they are automatic or appear deliberately, because we have consciously sought them in the depths of our memory, to give meaning to the contents that at that moment we have in our consciousness.

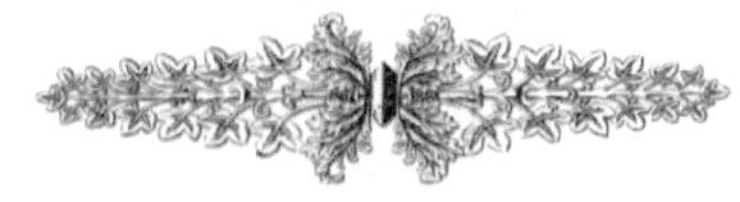

3. Observation

Within us are all the explanations that help us to clarify the truth; to detail the context and to define ourselves through all those thoughts that inform us of what we are.

Everything starts from there: our intentions, the reasons why we do something and all the explanations with which we try to understand the origin of everything that happens.

In our mind we try to look for the origin of what we observe, to know where it comes from, what are its foundations: the reasons why all those elements around us appear. In this way we find a purpose to every object we see; to every matter that moves through our consciousness.

It is a process that occurs automatically: just by perceiving each form we are already unconsciously analyzing its origin and its reason for being.

Thanks to this kind of contemplation, where we notice the characteristics of everything we observe, we can establish the usefulness of each object, of each experience we feel, when we are in contact with the world around us.

Your daily life develops under a surface in which it is not necessary to go too deep, it is enough for you to be attentive to external stimuli and to everything that comes to you from outside in order to solve most of the inconveniences that real life proposes to you at every moment.

You do not feel the need to go even deeper into yourself, nor do you have time to stop and observe that other reality inside you that also exists and is part of who you are.

You can attend to external demands without the need to think too much, without the obligation of having to observe yourself before making any decision; although all that other world, which also belongs to you, is still there.

Sometimes, when you stop to think for a moment and explore that which is beyond what you see, then you perceive that other dimension full of thoughts and ideas, of images and contents that move tumultuously inside your mind. Then you realize that you need to establish an order, to look for a greater "clarity" that helps you to understand all that world, and to separate yourself from everything that causes you confusion and leads you to incoherence, moving away from what you understand to be your true path.

If you manage to put the focus on that inner space where you find yourself, you will have the advantage of observing everything from a different point of view, which will make you see things more clearly and having the possibility of separating those toxic ideas or thoughts that drag you down unwanted paths, which lead you to act inconsistently with "what you are", or with what you really pretend to be.

In those moments is when you find the value of your own observation, of the benefits of meditating frequently and stopping to distance yourself from the mental noise that imprisons you and everything that leads you to an unexplainable emptiness.

Observing without labeling

There is a way to attend to all that surrounds us. It consists of doing it without using any type of thought. It would only be a matter of being in front of each reality, but without labeling it, without judging it, without passing it through the tapestry of our prejudices or any content that could suddenly emerge from our memory, related to what we have in front of us at that particular moment.

In this case, we would just be in front of things being aware of them, but without contaminating what we see, without resorting to any image of the past and without using our own language to pigeonhole our perception in a particular section.

In those moments we are free of all prejudice, because we will have freed ourselves from the thinking that often leads us to devise a reality that in no way resembles what really exists and is presented before us.

It is the best antidote for all those toxic thoughts that often flood us. The mere fact of observing them makes them lose their strength and go unnoticed, one after the other, without trapping us in this way.

You also get, at any time you decide, to select those contents that you consider more convenient depending on the circumstances in which you find yourself in each case.

Conscious observation

Connecting with ourselves is not so easy, we must be in a state of stillness that allows us to pacify our mind. So that all those thoughts that are executed in a mechanical way, cease to emerge with such persistence when we are in a state of peace and silence reigns outside and inside us.

From that point it is possible to reach that mental space, proper to the consciousness, where there is an absence of mental images and other contents that arise from the unconscious. Just when we reach that place, which is a moment where time stops and there is no other distraction coming from the outside to distract us, we can observe ourselves with total objectivity, free from the influence of thoughts.

In such a case, we feel close to the truth of things, and a deep wisdom spreads over us that makes us see the immensity of what we are, because in those moments we are aware of our true potential, as we are not contaminated by any toxic content coming from the mind, which confuses us or makes us see what we are not.

It is a way of observing yourself, away from mental noise and everything that can confuse your own vision of what you are. In this way you achieve a level of understanding of everything that has happened to you that you reach a level of knowledge about the past that you did not know before.

Until then you were only aware that you have had experiences that have marked you, but from this form of observation, you manage to analyze those events that happened in another way, much closer to the truth. This allows you to make a new reading of your own past, of those things that affected you for many years, making you the person you are now.

We only observe a part

We always have an inclination to attend only to that which interests us, which causes an attraction in us or dazzles us for some reason. It is usual for us to leave aside everything else, that which has no charm or attraction; or some inducement that seduces us enough to capture our interest.

We do not usually stop in each and every one of the details of what we observe; so that we only capture what catches our attention, because the stimuli have been very intense and we have stopped to observe them assimilating with it all the related information.

There are facts, actions that happen before us, that we hardly stop to contemplate, to consider if what we are witnessing has a reason to be, or a consequence that somehow affects us later on.

They are contents that we see but that we do not really weigh enough; they pass before us without us passing a judgment or a qualification that would allow us to attribute a sense or a concrete meaning to them.

We only retain part of the information we perceive, so we do not fully benefit from all that is in reality, since we only value what we can analyze at a given moment; although there are always some elements outside that, although we do not estimate them, are also perceived and incorporated into our memory.

Later, with the passage of time, they will appear related to some content that at a given moment we are paying attention to because it has some interest for some reason.

Not everything we perceive has a meaning for us. Sometimes, we simply absorb it and store it so that we can later relate it to some subject or theme that attracts us.

Faced with all this exposure to external materials that, in reality, in the end, are shaping our knowledge, one sometimes does not become very aware of all the knowledge that we can discover if we learn to extract what is important from all that we observe.

We could not quantify the value of everything that we do not appreciate but that we understand is also there, around us, ready to be understood and to be incorporated into our own knowledge.

The small details

When we are aware of everything in our immediate context, we perceive even the most insignificant elements in greater detail, keeping what we consider relevant. Later, thanks to all these new contents, we can reach an objective analysis of all that we have noticed on the outside.

Our thoughts obey, in a certain way, to all those small details that we have been writing down in our memory, when we have examined what surrounds us, when we have looked scrutinizing each reality, each component of what we have had in front of us.

They are the expression of that which is manifested in our consciousness, coming from our memory. They are the externalization of all those contents that we have been including throughout time in our memories; a clear manifestation of every experience we have lived, of every object we have observed and of every event we have noticed when we have looked around us paying attention.

All the concepts and notions at the time of valuing an opinion, are born from there, from all those judgments that are nothing more than the fruit of everything that our reason has been making sure of every little detail that we have appreciated in the external, visible world, in that palpable universe that has enveloped us at every moment.

Every episode we experience is not a mere incident that passes by without affecting us. Every set and affair that involves us will influence in one way or another our judgments, our way of reasoning and the purposes that we calculate in the future.

Behind every episode, every situation, there are circumstances that make it happen. It is up to us, through our capacity of observation, to find out those elements: those small details that form the circumstances of each situation, of each matter that arrives.

In fact, our intelligence also develops on the basis of that background that we accumulate over time, where our experiences are included and everything we have learned in our daily actions, through our behaviors and all those events that we have had the opportunity to experience and that are shaping, little by little, our circumstances.

BENEFITS

This form of observation allows everything to remain on the surface, and you are a witness, in some way, of everything that happens deep inside yourself. You access something like a distanced consciousness, where your energy is only limited to contemplate what may arise from the silence of that emptiness, which is free of memories and all those tensions that you usually feel in your daily activity.

In those moments it is as if you were returning to yourself; you feel that nothing can stop you. It is like an open door, silent, that opens inside you and once you enter through it you are flooded with a "conscious clarity", in which all your doubts disappear and you feel a relaxation that gradually absorbs you in a cloud of inner stillness, which makes you reach the center of yourself, which is beyond time and space, as it can only be accessed through this state of meditation, where your energy is only focused on that point, without the need to make any effort.

When this happens it is as if you enter into another dimension; as if you leave aside the action and take the path of contemplation, in a world different from the real one, where little by little your consciousness is moving away from everything that hinders and distracts you, and from all those elements that influence you and make you live immersed in an existence dominated by automatic thoughts, and conditioned by a series of habits that force you to repeat over and over again the same behaviors.

This way of observing places you in another dimension, in which you are much more aware of everything that happens inside you; so that you can reach a level of consciousness that allows you to attend to everything that interests you from another approach, from another way of seeing things very different from how you have perceived them in the real world, through the experiences you have had throughout your life.

What you think will no longer be so important, because you will stop identifying yourself with what is going on in your mind. You will be more focused on trying to be present in each moment, to live each experience without trying to force anything, without the need to look for explanations for everything.

You are more objective

You get to see things from a privileged position, we could say, from which you observe everything with much more objectivity, from a position much closer to the truth; since this other way of looking at reality is clean of any prejudice, it is far away from the toxic and repetitive thoughts that daily fly over your consciousness and come from your unconscious, which becomes visible through this mechanism of repetitive thoughts and impulses that you cannot control because you are immersed in a series of frequent habits that have become entrenched in you over time, based on repetitions of behaviors and patterns of behavior that you have been creating without being very aware of the consequences they entail, and the influence they come to have on your own destiny.

It provides you with a new vision of reality that is much more objective and closer to "what everything is", which helps you to perform more effectively in the world, with everything you do and with the kind of relationships you establish with those around you.

You will understand that through relaxation and serene observation, your analysis of things becomes more objective, and that everything that hurts you evaporates, it will go away if you do not let yourself be carried away by the mind and by all those thoughts that are reborn again and again automatically, that lead you to a repetitive existence where you are barely aware of the present and you barely have time to find the right answers to each situation.

Observing yourself, from the inner calm, has as a consequence a greater coherence between what you think and the acts that you finally end up doing. The fact of being able to establish in time a pause in your own thoughts, entails to be able to reach the control of these, so that you are the one who in the end decides the content and the frequency of appearance of each element that tries to occupy a space in your conscience.

It helps you to transform yourself

The fact of being able to stop your mind and start observing in a conscious way everything that happens, makes you find a suitable basis for your own transformation.

It can be a means to find the orientation of your own life again; to take control in a total way; to find calm; a means to find the right answers and all that truth that has remained hidden in you over time.

This capacity of observation, together with an adequate state of stillness, will also allow you the option of modifying some ideas and thought structures, and even beliefs, with which you are not very happy or simply wish to change because you do not find sufficient utility in that kind of content.

From here, you have the opportunity to make a much more real and objective analysis of yourself, which will lead you to modify many premises and beliefs you had about what once happened to you.

All this will lead you to a personal change, to modify many of the perspectives you had about your previous experiences, to value differently many of the relationships you had previously with other people close to you.

Possibly it will also lead you to change many erroneous thoughts about those people with whom you have had some kind of contact before, thanks to the acquisition of this new way of observing what is already in you, which remains stored in the depths of your inner world.

Therefore, thanks to the possibility of being able to observe our own thoughts, we acquire the ability to modify them according to the interests we have at any given moment.

You begin to understand that behind everything there is always a background, a double meaning. You come to perceive the true nature of what you look at closely. The result is another way of living; another way of being before everything that surrounds you.

Helps you resolve conflicts

Sometimes, conflicts assail you and annihilate you little by little in a wild process that leads you towards a perverse slope, in which you lose your balance and your peace is interrupted by a restlessness that little by little envelops you, leading you to anguish and discouragement.

And the fact is that there are thoughts full of senselessness, that lack a concrete purpose and that certainly do not contribute anything to personal transformation.

We may not know very well where they come from, but what is certain is that they break our internal balance, removing that slight harmony that we sometimes achieve when we remain silent, without feeding our mind with thoughts that trap us in uncertainty.

In order to modify them, it is necessary to look away from all those images that lead us to misfortune and that in most cases are automatic and are linked to a terrible feeling of unhappiness, which spreads irrationally throughout our knowledge.

The observation of ourselves should serve for that: to eradicate all those contents of our mind, which sometimes stagnates when it feels contaminated or works in an automatic way, without finding the way to stop this sometimes compulsive movement that tortures us with imaginary thoughts devoid of any logic.

When you observe everything from the calm, there is a deep acceptance of everything that happens around you, so that every difficulty does not feel like a threat, you just observe and identify everything that happens.

You can witness all this from the calm, without having to analyze anything. You only need to abandon yourself in silence, making sure that you focus your attention on what is happening inside that place in your mind where the memories of your memory spread: all that knowledge and that stored knowledge that live inside you and remain hidden until a certain task awakens them and they begin to occupy a space in your consciousness where they become images that lead you to elaborate ideas and beliefs that link you with the world and that determine who you are.

Achieving this, you certainly reach another level of life. You cease to be affected by everything that previously caused you suffering and discomfort, because you learn to minimize the importance of everything that is unnecessary.

These are the reasons why it is convenient to observe yourself frequently, to penetrate into that other dimension that is in you but that remains dormant because you do not usually enter.

You establish a distance

The division between what we think and ourselves, as observers of that which appears in our consciousness, allows us to establish a distance with our own thoughts and with everything that appears in our mind, which in many occasions are unwanted elements since they arise automatically and repetitively from the depths of our unconscious.

Thanks to this distancing we can achieve that the contents of the thought do not affect us, in such a way that thanks to this separation we can cancel the emotional charge of each element that comes to our mind.

Thus, with the passage of time, if we limit ourselves to observe them and let them pass, they will begin to cease to have value for us and will fade away without having any influence on our actions; they will gradually fade away until they cease to be repeated and lose their relevance within the hierarchy of frequent thoughts that continuously inhabit our consciousness.

This is the only way to gain control of what is happening within ourselves. It is achieved through observation, in those moments where there is only silence and a sense of stillness takes over your inner world, giving you control of everything that happens there.

It is something that can be learned through continuous practice, so that you can become, in this way, the master of yourself, of your most immediate impulses and of all those repetitive habits over which you barely have control and that undoubtedly are marking your own destiny, because they are the basis of everything you do daily in an automatic way, without being very aware of it.

4. Meditation

One form of observation is meditation, which is a technique that allows us to observe the course of our reason; a way to seek lucidity and harmony in all that we do not understand, to seek a meaning to all those concepts that have an effect on us.

When you look at your inner world, you observe your mind and the thoughts that occur there. When you manage to establish that process of seeing what is happening inside you, you are actually using meditation, which in a way means observing thoughts; for others it may mean something else, but the fact of being present, seeing how your mind works, attending to what is happening there, is like being in another state different from the normal one. You place yourself in a position from which you access a space that is reserved only for those who stay away from the noise and everything that can distract them from the outside.

One always seeks to meditate on what one's own imagination dictates, any reflection is welcome when you try to delve into it to obtain greater knowledge; through a consciousness that makes you see the reason, know the origin and causes of what you are trying to understand. It is the only way to arrive at a sensible discernment about all that we see and feel.

It is a way of giving importance to that which is useful, a way of daring to inquire into that which is not seen; to pry into the details of each element that surrounds us, looking for the details that lead us to the beginning and the essence of what really matters: all those components that are the foundations where we support ourselves; where the motives and every judgment we make begin; where the causes of the script we follow every day are; when we circulate in the world in connection with others.

It is a way of relating to oneself, an exchange of views between the person you are not and the person you have always been.

Meditation is a dialogue that facilitates the entrance to a hidden dimension that exists within us, in which we can observe the brightness of what we have always been and the darkness of what we do not want to be: of all that which causes us confusion and incites us to confront ourselves; in a non-stop struggle that only stops when we capture that space of silence that exists in our mind, when our consciousness has no intention, when there is no image or idea that aims to project us towards an objective, determined end.

Meditation can push you to search in that other side of your mind, those other deeper and more rational thoughts that have to do with you.

It can help you to tune into that channel where you can transform yourself and move away from all those divisions that appear and alter your psychic well-being.

It is like connecting with another source of different energy, through relaxation and the maintenance of a calmness that leads you to eliminate all those tensions that flow in your daily life and that little by little accumulate, to the point of making you explode in some moments, when you reach the limit.

Some admit that meditation is nothing more than focusing on a thought, focusing on a mental content, on an image without leaving it. I am more inclined to understand meditation as mere observation of what happens in that space that is your consciousness, both when there are thoughts and when there are no thoughts; being aware of every idea, every image that comes to you and also attend to those moments when there is no thought or anything that drags you or distracts you and takes you away from that moment.

What we get

Through this practice we can become aware of everything that happens both externally and within ourselves, since it gives us a capacity of observation that we were unaware of before, because this way of attending to any external or internal stimulus gives us the ability to take into account all the details that usually go unnoticed in our daily lives.

It is a way of being aware and awake, being witnesses of what happens in our own mind, which is the key to our functioning, because what happens at a mental level -all those thoughts that arise from our memory- is what leads us to act most of the time in an unconscious and automatic way; unless we know how to put a stop to all that endless train of automatic images that appear in our consciousness, one after another, without hardly having time to stop and pause to know how to calibrate at all times the consequences of following or clinging to a particular thought or focus on a particular mental content.

This other form of observation, if we understand it from this perspective, can help us to change our way of being in the world, to face life and the problems that arise in it in a different way, because it provides us with a way of being and being much closer and conscious, more conducive to face the problematic situations with more realism and awareness, so we get to be closer to the solutions than to increase these difficulties; that sometimes imprison us and generate a discomfort that we prolong in time, that make us enter in an endless loop from which we hardly have options to get out of.

All this can provide us with this form of meditation, that as we practice it we will be able to observe small achievements in our way of thinking, observing and controlling ourselves.

These achievements will then translate into greater psychic well-being, since they will serve to know how to discriminate at all times those toxic contents that take us away from the path we should follow to feel good about ourselves.

We will see results in a very short time, because our way of thinking in the end ends up making us "what we are" and what we show outside, in what we do, in our attitude towards life and the other people around us. All this will be reflected on the outside and we will be aware of it very easily.

This way of observing thought will take us to an other dimension unknown until now, it will lead us to enter more in contact with a knowledge and information about ourselves that most of the time has remained hidden, but that has always been there and that has to do with all that we are, with our "true purpose", with what is our essence.

It allows us an encounter with ourselves that will help us to find the hidden truth of things. It is as if we were opening the door of mysteries and discovering the way to solve all those enigmas that have surrounded us and that have caused us suffering because we lacked sufficient knowledge to solve them in due time.

All that wisdom is already in you, what happens is that it remains hidden in a place that can only be accessed through this mode of conscious and leisurely observation, distanced from the mental noise and any other distraction of the external world.

Meditation can be a good mechanism to look inside yourself and observe the situation in which you find yourself at any given moment, which will be expressed by all those thoughts that you will find in your mind and that will arise automatically without you making an effort to make it happen.

If you know how to find the tranquility and observe that, in a few seconds you will begin to experience a transformation that will be propitiated by that observation of what is in your mind.

Simply by observing that information, in silence, a change begins to happen in you, because you feel that you take control of what is happening inside you; and at that moment all those automatic thoughts stop blooming and remain less and less time in your consciousness.

The rhythm of appearance of all those contents begins to be slower and slower, disappearing all those images that arise from your memory accompanying you all day long, through a continuous and almost unalterable sequence; meditation allows you to vary this whole process.

Altering this mechanism is only possible if it is done from inner calm, from a much deeper level, without the need to force anything, without having to make any movement so that all that mental flow is paralyzed. It simply begins to eliminate itself; it begins to clear your mind through silence.

It is a very valuable technique to see what is inside yourself and discover the person you really are, which may be different from the image others have of you.

It is good to get used to do a small daily meditation, to break a little with the monotony of always having to be thinking about the same thing, obligatorily.

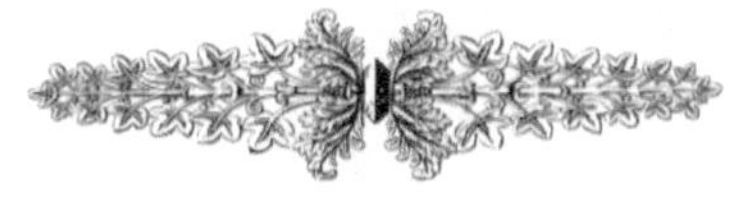

5. To be conscious

Consciousness is a concept that has many considerations. What I appreciate when I examine myself, within that reflection that I suggest everyone to do, is that there is within us a place full of images that are continuously reproduced and that we perceive internally. When that happens we are conscious of what we are thinking at that moment, we observe those reproductions as if we were in front of a screen watching a movie repeatedly, sheet by sheet.

At that moment we have a sense, a notion of what we are thinking, we come to understand with lucidity all that happens in our brain that gives us the ability to act with a purpose or a reason for being.

At this point we can say that the mentioned consciousness alludes to the internal perception that we have about everything that arises in our mind: such as judgments, ideas, reasoning and everything that our intelligence allows us to understand.

From this perspective, we could say that all the elements that appear in it are components of our memory, they are integral aspects of all those pieces that we have been saving over time. Many of those parts come together in fragments giving rise to ideas and beliefs, forming a block on which we then depend when establishing a judgment or giving an opinion on a given subject.

From another point of view, we can also consider consciousness as a process of our own mind in which there are no images, no figures from our own memory, and no other thoughts that occupy our attention.

It would be something like a space or a state without form, where there is a void that is not occupied by any appearance; as if it were a presence where there would be nothing, where we are only ourselves before that hidden reality in which there is no matter, no form. Let us say that this would be a second aspect of consciousness.

Therefore, in order to try to form an approximate idea of what it is, we must take into account these two considerations. So we could say that consciousness is that part of our mind that is composed of all those elements that arise from our memory and a space where all those forms dissolve giving rise to a void freed from images and the mental noise of thought.

To be conscious means to be awake, to be aware of all that happens not only around us but also in the deepest part of ourselves.

When you stay awake, you are a witness of the thoughts that circulate in your mind; you become aware, from within yourself, of your existence, of everything that conditions you and of the moment in which you live.

If you are conscious you will stop living in abandonment; you will get rid of listlessness, of apathy, because you will know how to defend yourself and protect yourself from everything that deviates you from "what you really are", from everything that takes you away from you, that arises unconsciously trying to disorient you, to convince you to keep trying to do the same things; that predisposes you so that all your actions are automatic, so that you barely have time to convince yourself that there can be another way of acting, another way of approaching reality.

To reach this, calm is also required: that peace in which you feel a certain conformity with everything that surrounds you, a tolerance and a conciliation with yourself that leads you to act with coherence, away from the ties of the external world, where sometimes you only find obstacles that prevent you from solving all those difficulties that gradually lead you to anguish and discomfort in the form of permanent sadness.

How to be conscious

The most important thing that happens to us occurs in that place of consciousness where we fix our attention, where we place our inner gaze. It is there that a struggle constantly takes place between the thoughts that arise unconsciously and ourselves, who are somehow separated from them, since we have the possibility of observing them, thus establishing a distance.

Generally, this struggle is won by the unconscious part, since it occupies the most space in your mind; although it is true that the other conscious part, in spite of occupying less space, can take total control and control the other part.

The latter happens when we are conscious and take control of our mind, deciding what we really want to do, what is in line with who we really are.

We are accustomed to follow, without reticence, everything that our mind proposes to us at every step, without stopping, even for a moment, to evaluate the consequences of following a certain approach, or to insist on an idea that is repeated incessantly in our consciousness.

In a way, this way of operating is nothing more than a consequence of our own nature. We do it this way because it is in our own human condition to act that way.

If you dwell too much on a certain problem, what happens most of the time is that the problem increases and solutions can hardly be glimpsed. Only when you somehow clear your mind of toxic elements that hinder "clarity", then is when you feel that you are in touch with the objectivity of things, you have less difficulty to observe the truth in them; when you get rid of mental noise and everything that comes from the depths of your unconscious, so that it clouds your objective view of things and takes you away from your true purpose, because it distracts you and leads you down other paths that deep down you do not want to go.

Only when you clear your mind of the unnecessary, you can become aware of what is happening inside you, of how to fill those voids in your consciousness in which there is no content and there is hardly any perception of time and space.

Thanks to this we can focus on a specific point, on a part, and through this choice we can delimit the contents that in each moment are present in our consciousness.

In this way we cease to be conditioned by thought, thanks to our own will and the ability to identify all those elements that appear in our mind.

This requires us to be conscious, to make an effort to enter into a state of stillness that allows us to clear a little of the thick forest that is our mind, to cultivate it and open paths that lead us along the path that best suits who we are, our true purpose.

This would be a way to put an end to all those dilemmas that exist within us, when we act without thinking too much about the consequences, or we allow our mind to work in an unconscious way, letting ourselves be conditioned by it.

It is worth making an effort to cross that barrier that exists between us and our own mind; in this way we will not be absorbed by it, it will become more rational and many things will cease to be a puzzle, we will not feel so paralyzed as often happens when we limit ourselves to always be seeing the same image, convincing ourselves that only that reality exists.

To be aware of all this you need to be awake, to live in the reality of consciousness, which is beyond what your mind is proposing to you at every moment.

Only if we clear our mind of everything that hinders us, that separates us from what we are, we will be able to observe with a conscious look everything that lies behind what we see, everything that lies beyond, everything that has caused each thing to be.

This can be achieved if we learn to connect with silence and with that stillness that only arises when nothing can distract us, separating us from that place where everything that overwhelms and destroys us disappears.

Sometimes, it is just a matter of observing, letting thoughts flow through your mind, not being influenced by any of them, allowing them to appear and at the same time disappear without affecting you in the least.

In fact, that is what we are talking about when we talk about observing your own consciousness, in those moments in which you manage to reach a stillness, through silence, that allows you to have control over everything that happens in your mind.

Thanks to our own will and other qualities that we also possess as human beings that we are, we can manage to establish a direction over this mechanism that we have embedded since we are born. To achieve this, we must remain conscious especially in those moments in which we lose control more easily, in those moments in which we let ourselves be carried away by those thoughts that deep down we do not want to have, but that emerge because we have repeated them with great assiduity, by habit, or because they simply obey desires that we want to realize but that in the long run are toxic for us, because they do not lead us to anything or solve any problem, apparently.

Everything depends on the degree of consciousness that we manage to reach. It is evident that the more we practice this way of facing what our mind can propose to us, the closer we will be to achieve this independence, as observers that we are, of all that structure of unconscious contents that arise to our conscience many times in an uncontrolled and repetitive way, without us being able to do anything to avoid it.

In order to approach the knowledge of all that which is produced in our mind, we must be conscious, trying to be always in a state of alertness, noticing everything that appears in our consciousness in the form of thought.

It is necessary that we look at our own reflections about everything that happens to us, in the reasoning and considerations with which we try to justify our most frequent affirmations, which are transformed into beliefs in many occasions far from common sense.

BENEFITS

Becoming conscious is the best way to discover what we really are. It is the best way to understand ourselves, to understand everything that happens around us.

All that we are is beyond what we see. It appears hidden inside ourselves, obscured by our own thoughts, by everything that floods our mind, that invades our consciousness in such a way that it takes us away from our true path, which is nothing more than the purpose for which we have come to this world.

From here you begin to be guided by what you are, not by what your circumstances and past experiences have made of you, which in reality is what is at the base of your thoughts; which are the ones that make you act in a certain direction, unless you are the one who takes control in a conscious way and takes control of everything that happens inside you.

It is the only way to be yourself, to be faithful to "what you are", which has more to do with that conscious part than with the other, with that which is formed by your automatic and unconscious thoughts.

It will certainly give us another vision of things. This way of understanding our mental functioning leads us to get in touch with our own consciousness, to know it in a more precise way. It leads us to the knowledge of ourselves, of everything that is hidden within us; it leads us to a wisdom that gives us that peace that is only possible when one reaches the full knowledge of "what is", when one comes to detect where exactly this knowledge is, how to access it.

Thanks to the level of consciousness that we can reach, through this new way of understanding what we are -through the knowledge of ourselves-, in this permanent contact with our own inner self, we will have access to a new way of understanding our own reality and that which surrounds us and that which we observe in the world that exists in our environment and with which we have close contact.

We will reach the transformation of ourselves through this new tool that is the use of our own consciousness to discriminate, within ourselves, those elements that are more related to "what we are" and what we understand to be the real truth of things, which can only be discovered when we strip them of all that is superficial, of what obscures their essence.

When we go deep inside ourselves to observe all that arises in our own mind, we become aware of all that infinite richness that lies within us, which is only visible if we know how to contact that other part that is hidden, but that always remains there, hidden, waiting to be observed and used.

In fact, that is where our true wealth lies, because that part of us has to do with what we really are, because it is not contaminated by that area of the mind composed of repetitive and unconscious thoughts.

When we are truly conscious, we come to distinguish what is part of us from that which does not belong to us because it has come to us from outside and we have assimilated it without hardly realizing it.

What is really part of us is everything that is far from any external influence, that has nothing to do with what has come to us from the material world. What we really are, truly, is at a much deeper level, away from thoughts and any label.

Becoming aware of your own thoughts leads you to the knowledge of everything that happens inside you. Thanks to this you can reflect and take into consideration all those aspects that you understand that are important; you can carry out a meditation through which you observe what is inside you, noticing all that information that has to do with yourself, where you can find an explanation to your behaviors, and clarify all those entanglements that life has led you to, through your own experiences.

From the depths of yourself you get to grasp the present, to establish a distance with the external world, not letting yourself be carried away by everything that your mind dictates; where you accumulate information that comes from outside, that reminds you that you have to behave like the crowd, like all those who surround you in your immediate context.

It barely leaves you a space to be you, so you can find yourself and eliminate everything that has nothing to do with your personality, with that deep dimension in you where you find your "true self", which never changes despite the influences and external circumstances, which constantly try to trap you at a high speed.

It is then when you begin to perceive beyond, when you acquire the true knowledge, which is only given when you are conscious and do not let yourself be dragged by that continuous movement of your mechanical mind that never stops flowing.

It leads us to control

Being conscious leads us to control, and that is what drives us to change; that change that we have often desired but have not been able to achieve because we lack the necessary knowledge.

Reaching that control means mastering our own thoughts, and everything that arises from our automatic mind that makes us not be ourselves; that we wander without being awake at many times.

In this sense, to be conscious implies to reach a control of our own mind, specifically of that part of the consciousness where thoughts appear; and of that other part where there is no image, no content or any form that occupies that space, giving rise to a consciousness without thought, even if it is in a momentary way.

When you are conscious everything stops, your problems no longer turn out to be such, because you learn to take the direction through that stop propitiated by the stillness itself that helps you to distance yourself, to not identify yourself with any thought that arises from the deepest part of your memory.

Once we reach that point we can lead ourselves, thanks to our will, wherever we want, with the advantage that we are totally conscious in every moment, and that we are away from any influence of our unconscious, so that we are no longer guided by all those immediate impulses that guide us continuously and to which we are accustomed.

If we learn to exercise this control over ourselves, over all that part of the consciousness where all those images that constantly flood us arise, our vision of reality will change, since we will have the possibility of observing in more detail that which can influence us most, so that thanks to this conscious attention we can transform it, change it for other contents that we understand that are more in accordance with what we are, with our "true essence".

The learning of this mechanism can be obtained through continuous practice; in this way we will achieve great results in the short term.

In reality, everything that happens inside us is what we allow to happen; so that, if we do not stop and do not pay attention to the nature of our own thoughts, in the end we will become someone who allows himself to be guided by his own mind without having his own autonomy, without having a will that allows him to act by himself by performing those acts that deep down he wants to put into practice.

Thanks to the observation that we can exercise on ourselves, we will realize this whole process and how to transform it into a new mechanism that frees us from the constant bondage of being constantly at the mercy of our own thoughts without being too aware of it.

Only in this way we will be able to pave the way for a "new consciousness", in which we are able to separate all that mental noise in the form of thoughts that floods us, thereby achieving a control over ourselves that allows us to act according to what we really want to do, leaving aside what our own mind proposes to us at every moment, regardless of our own will.

Thanks to the emergence of this new consciousness, our growth will be even better, because it will increase a higher level of presence in everything we do. From us will spring up an interest in expanding and enlarging all that we carry inside and that we barely prolong outside, because of that constant and unyielding attitude of closing ourselves in ourselves to remain continuously in a long darkness.

You connect with your own Being

To be conscious is to connect with your own Self; it is to try to conduct yourself with greater coherence, without the need to cling to every thought that pops up in your mind; it is to give yourself a space to meditate, to be able to identify the person you have become during all this time; it is to reconcile with yourself and abandon the confusion that may exist around what you should do in life.

When you are conscious a new movement begins towards you, where you learn to become what you really are; to stop living in the past and to follow the path of what you should do.

A bridge of communication opens up with something deeper within you -which has remained dormant until that moment-: a space where your "true nature" is found, where you learn to live in the present without the need to judge it.

Thanks to this you can go deeper, live a new experience within yourself, through which you can have a contact with a deeper dimension that encompasses everything, where you meet yourself beyond reason and the logic of the mind.

If you take that leap you will have the opportunity to propel yourself beyond, to move towards that place where everything stops, where your mind ceases and there is only an inner movement provoked by an energy that flows like the water of a canal that never stops or stagnates on the shore.

IF YOU ARE NOT CONSCIOUS

On numerous occasions throughout the day, we go astray, we lose direction without being very conscious of it. We get confused in a whole series of external stimuli and unconscious impulses that make us deviate from ourselves, from what we really are, and we forget the most important thing: what is happening in our own consciousness.

Most of the time we live in unconsciousness; it is our automatic mind that exercises its control over us and subdues us to the point of making us act in an uncontrolled way, with hardly any control over our own will.

In the end, we end up being the result of unconscious thoughts, which guide us without us realizing it, towards what we do not really want.

We become, therefore, the fruit of our own mind most of the time; the consequence of everything that has come to our consciousness from our memory, which is where the memories of all that we have lived, that we have experienced throughout our life are kept.

If you are not conscious of what you do, you will never be able to venture: to try another way of doing things; to try to undertake new initiatives that make you approach life in a different way.

If you are not conscious, you are absent from yourself, you will depend on your mechanical mind, which in most cases is irrational, it only follows the logic of repetition, distancing you from the knowledge of "what really matters"; of that knowledge that is only accessible when you go a little further, when you get to the source where the origin of what you are is and your "true nature" manifests itself, beyond the limits of the mind, where you reconcile with your own existence and find a new language to find expressions and concepts that remained hidden and meaningless until that moment.

You will never be able to ask yourself your "true purpose", which you can only discover if you go into the deepest part of yourself, where you find your authentic reason for being, where you can feel and perceive what you are and what each thing is. Only there you will be able to be present, without having the need to imagine or dream with invented ideas that run through your mind without any reason, which then drown when you look at the reality of life.

6. Inner space

Whenever you observe yourself, from inner calm, you do it from a point that is beyond your mind; you do it from an inner space where there is a void and the source where everything originates, from which you can look at every form that appears in your consciousness.

That inner space is like your temple: an inner world where you can enter through silence to set aside time and meet yourself, without the need to go back to the past; thoughts will stop moving back and forth when you begin to be aware of it.

Within that deeper level of consciousness is this other dimension, which appears when you enter that formless, thoughtless interval. When that happens, you feel that you have total control over your mind and over yourself, because at the same time that you have the possibility to observe everything that may arise in that space, you also have the opportunity to go into that silence, into that in-between, to carry out a much deeper exploration.

It is a source of wisdom where you find yourself, where you find your true self and you have contact with "what you are", with your authentic self and with everything that is not contaminated by the mind, by thoughts.

It is a space where you are alone with yourself and you discover your "true essence" and your true self. Thanks to this, any thought that emerges from your mind will not be able to affect you, since as you observe it, its strength diminishes; it is a way to appease its energetic charge, the influence that it can exert on you, forcing you to take action.

Once you take possession of that place, you move to a new reality closer to evidence, to authenticity. It will always be favorable for you since it will be related to the truth and not to all those erroneous beliefs created through toxic contents coming from your mind and all the information you constantly submit yourself to, without pausing to observe yourself and be aware of all this happening inside you.

Immediately you realize that there is no chaos there, but a tremendous harmony, that everything that arises from there does not affect you, as do the monotonous thoughts that are born from your unconscious mind. It is as if you were separated from any emotion, which you also have the capacity to observe in those moments, within that space in which nothing exists, but at the same time everything that you are and what you can become is concentrated.

We can also observe it

Everything that appears in your mind is fleeting, but that which is beyond, in that space freed from thought, is permanent, it is not subject to time, nor does it disappear as do the forms that arise in your consciousness, which you can easily expel if you dwell on them and do not label them or judge them.

It has nothing to do with any fiction of thought, nor does it repeat itself as do many images in our mind, which refuse to disappear unless you examine them carefully in a process of meditation, in a calm way, through silence.

What happens in that space also becomes visible and we can come to observe it; it is stable, for it is not subject to the knowledge that comes from our memory; it is something that blossoms from deep within ourselves and is stripped of time.

HOW TO ACCESS

To live in the mind is to live in a continuous war, where you always have to be moving, obeying thoughts that become visible and that determine what you have to do in each moment, that consume your energy as they appear and disappear.

They only stop if you go a little deeper, if you let yourself be abandoned and turn all that mental noise into silence; then your energy is transformed following another sequence that leads you to another more secluded place: another world where you begin to live a new experience, which frees you from everything you have encountered so far in your mind.

When you try to disconnect from your most habitual thoughts to move to that much deeper level, where the mental noise does not have so much influence on you, your mind offers a resistance that forces you to stay in that superficial state, in which thoughts are repeated over and over again, so that in the end everything ends up in an action related to those thoughts that are grouped one after another in a mechanical and unconscious way.

It is not easy to make the leap to this other level of consciousness, where there is a change of focus: it is no longer the thoughts that direct you, but you are the one who becomes the observer of all those contents that appear in your mind.

Thanks to calmness we can enter into all that hidden knowledge, which arises when your mind is cleared of all that succession of mental contents that constantly try to open a hole in your consciousness.

It is an abrupt journey, because you have to protect yourself from the spell of thought and the anguish of some emotions, such as sadness, which often oppresses and dominates you, changing your focus of attention to another place.

To make that movement that can move you to your inner space, it is necessary to practice calmness, because it is the only thing that can help you to join that place where nothing can distract you.

If you use your awareness while being present, then you feel how most of the useless thoughts evaporate and you begin to abandon yourself in silence. You notice how all the usual activity of your mind subsides; it is as if you were alert, but without being active, as if you let yourself be carried away by that empty interval where no thought arises and no image appears.

When you are conscious you just observe, feel your breath. If you keep stillness, if you look at how your mind works, you will get to the beginning, where every thought, every idea, reason and all those emotions that make you feel a certain way and that drag you without you realizing to think in a particular direction.

Then you begin to listen to yourself, as you have rarely done; and when you start to look at yourself from that place, you conclude that something very powerful is inside you that makes you see reality with another look, in a conscious way, without the need to react to every stimulus as you usually do in a normal situation.

Only in a state of relaxation you can get in touch with that space inside you from which you can glimpse all that occupies your consciousness, that comes from your memory and that arises automatically through thoughts and images on which you focus your attention without being very aware of it.

In moments of stillness you can get in touch with that other part of yourself where "what you really are" is, which is not contaminated by any thought or content from the past.

You come to realize that you are in contact with that place when the noise of the mind fades and your repetitive thoughts stop invading you, when it seems that everything is flooded with a silence that makes you evade any external distraction.

At that moment you feel that you are fully concentrated in that part of your interior in which you begin to glimpse an emptiness that at the same time makes you feel an inner peace that you cannot experience with anything else in the external world, in the material world.

This is possible because in that space of "no mind" there is the right pause to take control, to become in control of your own thoughts. In such a case, it is you who guides your own mind and not the other way around; it is not the mind, in those moments, that leads you.

You take control because you have managed to establish a pause and you have been able to remain in that space where there is only stillness and silence and the mind does not invade you with its usual automatic thoughts that distract you and take you away from what you really are, from your true self, from your essence.

In such a situation, you can stay as long as you wish, although the usual functioning of your mind leads you to always remain in that normal state in which thoughts emerge mechanically and you let them lead you, following them to the place where they want to take you depending on the objective they have in each moment.

With practice, the moment will come when it will not cost you any effort to establish contact with that other deeper dimension that exists in you, in your inner world, where you learn to separate yourself from the mental noise and from everything that distances you from "what you are", coming from the material world, from the world of forms.

Through silence

The way to access that dimension from where you can observe all that happens in your own mind is by letting yourself be carried away by silence. It is not necessary to fix your attention on a certain point, it is about getting your mind to calm down all those automatic thoughts that are constantly arising in your consciousness.

This dimension can only be accessed if you free yourself from what is in your mind and take some time for silence to take over that moment and lead your energy into yourself. It is then that you begin to look in this other direction, forgetting what is outside; even though there is a flow of stimuli hitting you on the outside.

This only happens when there begin to be large spaces of silence between one thought and another. When this interval lengthens, you can control the direction and sense of the contents that arise later on.

That is why a few moments of waiting are required to achieve this mental silence between one thought and another. At that moment, you can decide what kind of contents will occupy your consciousness, the sense and direction you want to give them, depending on where you want to put the focus of attention.

In that intermediate, where silence reigns, you can take control of that space; as well as of everything you think or what you can come up with through the union of structures of thoughts that you can create from that place, in a voluntary and conscious way.

Once you get to that point, you will have moments when you feel the need to leave, because you are still not very used to have such a degree of observation, so you will feel the intention of wanting to get away from there; but thanks to the inner calm, if you use it in those moments, you can continue in that state - in that interval - for a longer time, so that it will help you to take control of the situation, without letting yourself be carried away by other kinds of thoughts that have the purpose of getting you out of that situation and start again to function normally, as you have been doing all your life.

WHAT YOU GET

Only if you move away from everything that separates you from your "true self", which is in that space without content of your consciousness, is when you get to find the genuine meaning of many questions that you have raised throughout your life and for which you have not had or have not found a timely response.

Everything takes on a different meaning if we strip ourselves of the conditioning of the mind and we choose to remain on that side of consciousness away from the noise and images that come from memory. Only in that space of "no mind", which is not flooded by thought or time, can you reconstruct all those experiences you have had and give them a new meaning very different from the one you gave them when you perceived them for the first time.

From your inner space everything is seen in a different way, much closer to "what you are", closer to the reality of things and to the truth, because all the objects and forms that appear there are not so contaminated by thought.

You can see that everything that is born from there is more authentic, because it is not contaminated by the usual contents of the mind, which are based on information that we acquire from the outside that is often incomplete.

Only in that space of silence you can take control of everything that happens inside you, so that you can redirect everything that happens in your consciousness, in a deliberate way, giving a sense and a meaning to all those things that before seemed incomprehensible or difficult to assimilate.

It is really when you take command of yourself, when you get to discover "what you really are", the true purpose of your existence.

It is like being in contact with a source of wisdom that allows us to solve in another way what we understand that for us is a problem. From this space we can become conscious, knowing that behind any difficulty there is a series of thoughts that we have organized and structured in such a way that they lead us to elaborate a series of erroneous conclusions that are transformed into toxic beliefs and emotions that make us think that a fact or a specific issue is a problem for us.

If we all learned to connect with that space, with that other dimension that exists within ourselves, we would have a much calmer attitude towards life and we would give value to what really matters.

Surely we would not let ourselves be dragged so easily by all those external stimuli that accompany us on a daily basis, by all those influences from the outside that confuse us and generate toxic thoughts that become part of a programming that ultimately ends up leading to unwanted habits.

If you practice this frequently, you will find other sensations, and a world that has been there, hidden for you, and that thanks to this becomes present; but without being subject to time, because once you place yourself in it, you do not feel the need to resort to the past or to evade thinking about the future. You do not feel the need to escape from that situation, on the contrary, you forget about any conflict that circulates in your mind and you only limit yourself to think about "what you are", without your consciousness being influenced by any other kind of thoughts.

You move away from the influence of the mind

Thanks to the inner calm you can observe everything that is hidden in the deepest part of yourself, everything that steals your energy and that you accept without further ado because you are used to do things in a mechanical way, without trying to know what is beyond yourself; so you create a system that does not allow you to penetrate beyond, to reach the depths.

A system that makes you act involuntarily, most of the time, always at the same pace, without you being aware that you can change it, that you can be above that state of mind and modify your way of thinking, through the use of calm and conscious observation.

To do this you must get to the "center" itself, which is separate from what usually happens in your mind. It only consists of letting yourself be swept away by silence and stillness, and letting your energy flow towards that other level of consciousness where there is no resistance and you come into contact with "the source", which envelops everything in a void that shuts out the sounds and noise of your own imagination.

Only if we are attentive to that space of our consciousness, which at first seems empty, we will feel free from the influence of the mind and anything else that tries to separate us from that instant, from that place where we find ourselves through an inner peace that floods us completely and that separates us from any stimulus that tries to break that stillness that is created in those moments in which you manage to control everything that happens inside you; particularly in your mind, in the flow of your own thoughts.

Only there you can manage to stay awake, to meet your "true self", in a conscious way, in a phase where all activity ceases and you do not feel any need to follow your mind.

In this dimension, which is far from thought and is where you meet yourself, you no longer allow yourself to be absorbed by the impulses that arise from your unconscious: by all that frenetic activity of images that circulate, spending your energy repeating always the same content, while you remain there, helpless, unable to change that process conditioned by all those expressions that appear in your mind, that do not allow you to be yourself in all circumstances and that make you remember in a constant way all the conflicts you have lived through and that sometimes you have had to repress to avoid being a slave of suffering.

You can only be aware of this reality if you do it from the calm, from that center that is inside you where there is a different stillness that leads you to mastery of yourself, without the need to force anything, keeping a distance from everything around you and that most of the time has prevented you from seeing the truth and everything that lies behind things.

If we reach the domain of that hidden world, where everything that clouds our understanding is turned off, we will be able to associate in a correct way everything that comes to our consciousness.

When your thoughts cease, your consciousness is abandoned in a vacuum where there is only a calm that somehow cancels all that mental activity that causes us so much internal noise: that apparatus of images and judgments that form all that din in the deepest part of ourselves.

When we come out of all that bustle, out of all that exposure of thoughts and unconscious impulses, we manage to glimpse the silence, which has always remained there, hidden, at rest, waiting for the occasion to become visible, to take us to another level in which we are the ones who observe all that happens inside, in those empty and secret spaces of our own consciousness, where stillness reigns and nothing can distract you.

To remain there, in that peaceful serenity, is to reside in the source from which everything begins, because before a thought emerges there is an emptiness, a space without thought, a silence that is not occupied by anything; it is what there is before the contents that occupy our consciousness emanate.

It is precisely at that point where "peace of mind" is reached, that calm that manages to cease your intellect and placate the constant repetition of reasoning and ideas that gradually fade away, thanks to silence, through the extensions of your mind.

If we remain for a while in that location, in that position of tranquility, we feel a peace full of harmony, which leads us to be in consonance with "what we are", thus achieving a sense of inner unity that we have never experienced before, in our experience with the material world.

It is only possible to reach that balance, that union with ourselves, from that redoubt, from that place that is your consciousness without form, without thought, without those mental images that arise repeatedly from the depths of your memory, that trap you automatically and guide your attention to other unwanted spaces.

In those moments, where there is only a deserted space and silence, you have the opportunity to be in front of the origin, to be in that point where everything is caused. All your ideas, your judgments and reasoning, germinate there, in that place where illusions, plans and beliefs, reflections and all your good intentions are created.

To place ourselves in that deeper dimension within ourselves, frees us from the deception of the mind, from that falsehood hidden in many thoughts that we observe in our consciousness and that insist on appearing again and again, trying to become visible at the slightest opportunity.

You reach the true transformation

It is there where the real transformation takes place, within yourself, when you free yourself from thought and become the person you always were, which has nothing to do with the mask or facade that you represent outside.

From there you can resume your true path, with which you have always identified yourself, because that is where your true objective starts, your vital goal, the purpose for which you came here and that sometimes you lose sight of because you get distracted by what you observe in the outside world, where silence ceases to remain and you begin to forget yourself, through false appearances in which you cannot distinguish the truth.

Your real development begins with your inner experience, when your actions coincide with what you feel you really are; when they are in line with your purpose and in consonance with your "true nature".

The real transformation occurs when you connect with your deepest self, in that other world away from the forms of thought, from the images of memory, which is in a more transcendent place, where the source of who you are is, where you feel at peace with yourself and your problems cease to exist and all that mental content that keeps you in a permanent struggle in which you always have the need to win and that makes you break your tranquility and do not enjoy life.

To place yourself in your space is to go back to the beginning. It gives you the opportunity to restart what you have lived; it gives you a time to turn your experiences into a valid instrument for your own development, to transform yourself.

Accessing this space, where you get to meet yourself, gives you a new attitude towards the world, another way of being different from those around you, from the difficulties you have to face daily.

You find your hidden potential

Therein lies all our hidden potential, which we cannot glimpse until we establish that contact with that part of us that remains asleep and to which we barely access, since we are more aware of the noise that comes from our own mind and all those automatic thoughts that invade us continuously, like an endless train that has no pause, that overtakes us and leads us to act in an uncontrolled and unconscious way, creating in us repetitive habits that are very difficult to get rid of and that lead us to an unwanted destination, which has nothing to do with the path we should follow to be ourselves at all times; to act in accordance with our "true essence", in a coherent way and adapted to what we really are, close to our own nature.

Encourage your creativity

Getting in touch with this other deeper level, which is within your own inner self, within that space of consciousness far from repetitive thoughts, makes you find yourself in a position where you feel the need to create new elements.

You observe that within that space there is nothing and you tend to fill it with your own elaborations, which you can weave together through components that you extract from all the information stored in your memory.

Unlike the normal functioning of the mind, on this occasion, this process occurs in a voluntary, deliberate way: you are the one who searches for the contents creating new structures of information related to a certain topic.

This voluntary creation of ideas and grouping of images and thoughts can lead you to elaborate a new reality different from the other one that is formed in your mind -most of the times unconsciously- and that later leads you to invent a series of erroneous beliefs that make you interpret the world in a wrong way.

When the information appears in a conscious way - within that creative space that initially is empty because it is not occupied by any thought-, all that you create keeps a greater consonance with "what you are", with yourself, and not with the character that your mind has created based on the information that springs unconsciously from the bottom of your memory.

7. Encounter with oneself

It is difficult for us to be ourselves at all times, since most of the time we let ourselves be guided by everything that appears in our mind and that in many cases has nothing to do with what we really are, which is something that is beyond our own thoughts, the mental content that comes from our memory.

When we delve into our inner world, trying to find our own identity, we often fail to find harmony: that wisdom that makes us look at things with a certain stillness in their right proportion, in consonance with ourselves.

We remain tied for a long time to a series of mechanisms that arise from our unconscious and take over our mind, and therefore ourselves, forcing us to be what we are not, to act in a certain way that has nothing to do with what we really intend to do; to continue on the path we think we should follow; to lead a coherent life in every way.

We live constantly in a state of alarm; although we remain still in one place, we continue being active, since our mind does not stop flowing, it does not stop for a moment and overwhelms us with one thought after another, causing that we do not have any moment of relaxation to take control of all that happens to us and that we cannot stop in any way.

All this is probably caused by the constant deterioration to which we are subjected because of stress; of our previous learning, in which we have been guided by a series of models that we try to follow and imitate and that are based on constant activity, in the daily routine.

We hardly have time to find ourselves, for our personal development, for a self-knowledge that can propel us towards the improvement of our own lives and to a greater knowledge of what we are and of all that potential that is hidden in the depths of our own inner self.

When we move away from the material world and we go deeper and fix our attention more on our inner space, we access a mysterious world for us, because we are not used to be in contact with that new environment where peace and silence reigns and you observe yourself as if you were a witness apart, distanced from what your own thoughts are, from what you perceive.

Once we get in touch with that other part, which is where "what we really are" is, we discover a knowledge that was there, hidden, without us realizing it before. It is an accumulation of knowledge about life and ourselves that arises suddenly, simply by having separated our gaze from what usually happens in our repetitive mind.

How it is achieved

Within our inner world we find ourselves, thanks to the observation we make of our own consciousness.

The knowledge of what we are comes precisely from there, from that act by which we are conscious of all that we think and perceive internally; of our existence; of our way of proceeding and of the rest of things that form our way of being: our way of conducting ourselves and of executing each action in the external world.

These are moments in which you realize that it is just about being and observing stillness, without the need to force anything, allowing the flow of those contents that arise sporadically from your mind and that little by little are calming down and decreasing their frequency as you just observe them; in fact, peace of mind is about that, keeping yourself conscious, but without thinking about anything.

You don't feel the urge to search for more thoughts -you think everything is fine as it is-; there is no need to label anything, to name anything; there is no obligation to turn to the past or to think about the future. At that moment there is no force that can dominate you; you are free from all influence, even from time.

In our mind flow an endless number of contents related to what we habitually do in our daily life. They are the ones that shape our habits: what we do repeatedly in many occasions without being very conscious of it.

All this material that takes over our mind leads us daily, allows us to act in the context in which we live, making us relate to our fellow men, especially with those closest to us.

But these elements, which occupy most of our mind all the time, do not allude to personal aspects that have to do with ourselves. These are in a different section, which can be accessed if we manage to stop these other thoughts that are more habitual and repetitive.

It takes a while to get to know yourself, let's say it is not something that is achieved overnight. It is a matter of looking at yourself, in a habitual way, to understand everything that is going on inside. It is just a matter of observing what you feel at every moment; your most habitual reactions and also what you normally do, which is what you end up becoming: what you repeat most easily is what forges your own destiny, even if you are not very aware of it.

The best self-knowledge is the one that comes from within. It does not take into account what others say, the people around you, or what you observe outside about what has to do with you. The best way to know yourself is to look at yourself, since all the keys are inside each and every one of us, what happens is that we do not see them because they remain hidden, hidden by those habitual thoughts that mostly have nothing to do with who we are.

All this knowledge can be acquired thanks to the discovery of all that there is in your inner world, which leads you to another vision of things much more conscious and calm, since you do it from a position in which you are hardly influenced by any external or internal stimulus.

To access it we must separate ourselves from what our mind is proposing to us at any given moment, because this has very little to do with what you are.

Going inside yourself is not so easy, it requires a daily practice if you want to do it easily.

It is complicated because we are used to living outside ourselves, in the external world. All our actions are performed outside and, by habit, we are accustomed to be more aware of the stimuli that surround us than of what happens inside us, in our inner world.

However, doing this practice is convenient, because you have a space to stop thinking a little and to situate yourself and thus regain your perspective, to take again the right direction of your actions and everything that goes through your head.

WHAT YOU GET

The encounter with yourself leads you to discover an inner reality that is in you and that is part of what you are and what you have been.

The knowledge of this new reality leads you to a wisdom that always leads you to seek the "clarity" of the things that pass through your consciousness, which often go unnoticed because our attention is focused on all those mechanical thoughts that come from the unconscious and that flood us at every step repeatedly and without us having control over them.

True knowledge is the deep knowledge that you acquire when you investigate reality from the deepest part of yourself.

You observe differently

Once you manage to connect with yourself, within yourself, you begin to observe reality in a different way, in a much more distant way. In such a way that many things that used to affect you stop affecting you; all those stimuli that usually capture all your attention and distract you very easily stop influencing you.

You can exercise control over everything you observe, both outside and inside yourself. In such a way that at any moment you can decide, consciously, the type of information you are going to pay attention to, and which contents you are going to leave in the background because you consider them irrelevant to you.

All this makes you keep a distance that helps you to see things objectively, without being affected by them. It is a good method to control emotions, since when you establish a distance between you and what you think and observe internally, you are no longer affected by the emotional charge with which many contents are accompanied, you are only influenced by what you pay attention to, what you follow in an automatic way, as if you were a robot, without making the necessary pause to glimpse the consequences of following a certain thought or an idea that ultimately ends in a repetitive action, which leads you to create habits that ultimately condition your life and your destiny.

From the knowledge of yourself everything is seen with a much more attentive look, which takes into account every little detail, which are also important and influence you in your way of being and feeling.

From this place, it is the best way to observe everything; through a conscious look, away from any contamination coming from the material world or from your unconscious mind.

You feel closer to who you are

It is the best way to always stay true to your "true essence", to what you have always been.

You will feel closer and closer to what you are, because thanks to this state you will find in your mind other kinds of contents that were previously inaccessible because they barely had space to stand out.

You will notice this slight change when you see how little by little other kinds of thoughts begin to be incorporated into your consciousness, which are charged with another purpose and with far fewer contradictions.

Then you will have the opportunity to perceive all those things that before appeared incomplete to you. Everything that in those moments is reproduced in your mind will have a clarity and a vividness that you will believe that everything comes from the same source, which perfectly summarizes what you are and contains all the necessary knowledge for you to achieve balance and your life returns to temperance, to inner calm, where silence begins and mental restlessness ends.

If we establish contact with "what we are", in the depths of ourselves, we will reach a profound change that we will experience very quickly, since we will be in communication with that "source" from which everything starts: the center where what we really are originates, from which we should never depart, where our "true nature" is found, the wisdom necessary for the solution to all our difficulties and with which we do not always have contact, since we remain distracted by all those external influences that take us away from that place.

He who finds himself and knows and observes himself, is on the right path, on the right road so that all his actions go in the same direction: the one that has to do with his true purpose and with what gives full meaning to his life.

It is a means to find your path, your true purpose, to know how you have to walk it; what are the steps you have to follow, what kind of ideas you have to reinforce to reach your goal (what you have initially set for yourself to lead a full life, without contradictions, to not betray yourself and always be faithful to your own beliefs and not to those who have tried to instill from outside).

You correct your mistakes

It is a way of seeing yourself acting in situations that have already happened, with the idea of being able to rectify many erroneous interpretations that at the time you made of what happened to you and that marked you without you realizing it in your later actions; that which made you the person you are.

Now you can modify all this from self-observation and through your own knowledge, investigating in your past, in those experiences that were more relevant to you and that influenced you in such a way that they definitely marked you, turning you into the person you are now.

From that self-knowledge you can re-evaluate if it was worth acting in a certain way in those moments where you decided to intervene and make a decision that led you down a path that led you to what you are today.

It is the best way to rectify and turn back; to look for solutions where there were none; to find explanations to what you did not understand in certain moments of your life where you needed more than ever a support and help that no one gave you; to find coherence to avoid many confusions that you find in your daily life.

If you do not know yourself, you will probably make many more mistakes when making some key decisions for your life. Only with the passage of time he realizes the mistakes made in the past. For this kind of people life is a learning by trial and error, they delegate in time and experience their own knowledge.

It is a way of looking at your past, but from a more objective perspective and closer to the truth. The knowledge of yourself makes you have another very different reading of the things that happened to you, which leads you to make a review of your past in which you can become aware of the moments in which you were not right when interpreting what has happened to you.

You cope with distractions

It is also a way to deal with the daily distractions that take you away from who you are, deep inside yourself, and what you want to become, what you want to build and develop through conducive habits.

You can focus on what is more in line with what you really are and what you want to do, managing to stay away from all those impulses that usually arise, without you barely realizing it, from the depths of your unconscious.

You reach a control of yourself that you did not know before, by which you manage to avoid suffering and that many things stop affecting you.

YOUR TRUE SELF

Your true self is your essence: what you really are. It is located in that part of consciousness where there is only an abyss of silence and calmness that leads you to find yourself, beyond the din from outside and the commotion of your ideas, which run through your mind in an impetuous way, capturing your attention and using your limited energy.

Your authentic self is found in that place of your consciousness isolated from the din, in that space without images that sometimes exists in your mind; where there is only stillness and a quiet pause in the spiral of ideas that travel within you endlessly.

It is there where you find the true source of what you are and what you will be. It is where you discover your authentic essence, at that point where time does not exist and space is only a hollow lapse of impressions.

There is no thought to identify it, for it is beyond the form of any mental content. It is removed from the images of the mind, and is not influenced by time. What we really are is beyond any idea, it is something that is separate from the structure of the mind, which is formed on the basis of everything that enters through the senses in our contact with the world;

when we relate, or simply observe everything that surrounds us daily in the context where we live.

It is a spring from which everything can emerge,
although apparently it is only a bottomless abyss. In
this place are gathered those expressions of memory
that you require, only those that you long for and not
those that your unconscious mind resolves, because it
is free from the link with any unwanted thought that is
born in a redundant and careless way from the bottom
of your memory.

All your essence is there, in the very heart of who
you are, far from the world of ideas; from the constant
visions of memory, which remains hidden in your
memory awaiting an exit to your consciousness, often
confused by the figures of the past and the projections
of the future that circulate in your mind continuously
throughout time.

The person who connects with his inner self discovers the meaning of the reality that surrounds him:
all those things that have made him the way he is. Everything acquires its true meaning, since you become
part of that space where you obtain all that knowledge
that has to do with yourself, and that you can only find
there, in that place where stillness reigns and no
thought can contaminate what is emerging in your
consciousness from the deepest part of yourself.

How to get there

When you reach that extreme where your mental
activity ceases and silence begins to flourish and you
stop acting, then you begin to "be" in that other world,
which in reality is the center where the true root of

what you are lies; of your "true essence", which has nothing to do with that character that is a product of your mind and of all the movement that occurs there, which conditions you and dictates the type of actions that you have to perform, through a constant movement of images that circulate through your consciousness coming from your memory.

The best way to reach that center where your true self is, is to make a separation between you and your own mind, observing the thoughts at a distance, establishing a separation between what you see and yourself, between the images that come to your consciousness and you in your position as an observer.

In this way we will manage to separate ourselves from any influence, both external and internal, that may distance us from what we are, that prevents us from being ourselves in every moment of our life.

It only consists of looking with purpose, with the will and the desire to find ourselves; far from our own reason, from our intellect, beyond the mind and all those judgments that constantly occupy us, that are the basis of our own destruction and the source of all those affections that we feel when we remain far from what we really are, from our "true essence".

Once we discover that empty space where silence reigns, we will be able to get in touch with what we are, we will realize that there is something beyond our own thoughts, beyond what we observe in our own mind, which is distanced, separated, from all those contents of our memory; they are elements that have to do with what you really are, with your true essence.

To be able to remain there, in our "true nature", it is necessary to delve into our own interior to discover that part of the consciousness that is not contaminated by thought and that is free from the noise that our own mind provokes through the incessant repetition of images.

You can get hold of that realm; and once you do, you will feel that you come to the government of your own inner self. It is the moment when you reach your greatest potential, because at that point you become aware of your true gifts, with which you have been endowed; you discover your "true self", surrounded by a peace that leads you to stay away from the distractions of the material world that constantly surround you and that keep you away from what you are.

8. Thought

Each sign that arises in our mind is nothing more than a reminiscence of the past, a vestige that is in our memory, that evokes a fact that we have already lived, that we have observed or learned before; that is why we recognize each memory, because it alludes to something with which we have already had contact; that is why we feel that there is a proximity, an identification with all those evocations that arise from the depths of memory and that we then observe on the screen of our own consciousness.

Thanks to thought we search for all that information that we carry within us and we propagate our ideas and beliefs, which have been created on the basis of our own interpretations of everything that has previously been exposed before us.

Through thoughts we can carry out affirmations; manifest ourselves on a certain matter; ratify our own conclusions and feed fantasies that we make persevere in time in order to lengthen some illusions.

Thoughts are different on each occasion; sometimes they can also be contradictory, opposite; many of them, in reality, are useless.

They are charged with a penetrating energy that occupies your whole mind, illuminating other similar thoughts, which begin to spring from an inexhaustible source and continue to reproduce themselves constantly.

What is thought

A thought is nothing more than a reproduction of what we have already seen before, which has multiplied in our memory by constantly repeating itself in our consciousness.

In our consciousness we perceive our own thoughts - however small they may be - which are nothing more than impressions that are impregnated on a blank screen, leaving an imprint that impacts on us, and once it arises we try to evoke it repeatedly if its effect causes us a certain impression.

Each thought is a representation of all those signals that are stored in our memory, it is nothing more than a sample of each and every one of the clues that our past has left us, that we have been experiencing over time through our own experiences.

A thought is actually a representation that is formed in our consciousness, thanks to some contents that remain in our memory and that at a certain moment have arisen and have become present in such a way that we get to observe them, checking how they spread through our mind.

A thought is the effect of our own learning, it is the product of all that we have come to know in our contact with the world.

It is the fruit of our perception, its final content, an image that we have previously captured and that, thanks to our imagination, we later transform into a concept, an idea or an impression that remains stored forever in the depths of our memories.

Thoughts are representations that are displayed in our mind as figures or symbols that have an easily recognizable form and appearance.

They form structures, and once they appear we know exactly what they refer to: their appearance is familiar to us; it is as if we have seen them before.

In reality, they are components that we have already observed before, so that once we perceive them in our consciousness, we immediately realize the meaning they have; we notice their meaning just by contemplating them once.

When several thoughts are united we arrive at understanding, to discern through the use of our reason. In this way we become aware of what we are, of our judgments and concepts that constantly fly over our mind.

Thanks to thoughts we reconstruct a reality that we have created inside ourselves, copying the scenes we have observed and interpreting the facts and every experience we have lived, which have helped us to describe reality in an understandable way; to reason through arguments, although sometimes these are contradictory.

It helps us to understand

Through thought we try to understand all our ideas, giving a sense to every approach we have and every approach; through which we have a perspective, a vision of things that makes us understand them when they appear before us.

Whenever we have a vision of something, a thought appears next that manifests itself to help us understand that presence that appears before us; it is an objective reality that also exists and has a reason for being, so we immediately try to make sense of it, as we do with any object, element or circumstance that we have before us.

Our thinking, therefore, has an intention. Sometimes its purpose is to help us to recognize all that we have around us, or what we observe within our own consciousness; another purpose is to lead us to action, since many contents have the intention of leading us to carry out a specific activity; so that, if they do not fulfill their purpose, they insist on repeating themselves over and over again until they achieve that aspiration, which is the idea with which they are born and spring from our mind.

Therefore, thoughts aspire to help us interpret the world: that you come to understand everything you see so that you can interact in this way with everything around you. That is why they permeate your mind; sometimes without any kind of filter and achieving such fascination in you that you let yourself be fooled by that constant whisper of one image after another on the screen of your own consciousness, so that you can not escape that runrun that strives to steal your attention and shake you inside so that you end up moving; although in many occasions you do it without having a fixed direction, without a purpose.

Constant movement

There is always the inner need to be thinking, to be immersed in judgments, concepts and words that penetrate your consciousness from your memory.

It is difficult not to think about anything; by our very human condition we are designed so that our mind is continually in action, so that we are accustomed to be constantly pondering one thought after another, even when we are performing a concrete action. In such a case we can keep our thought focused on what we are doing; or we can be, at the same time, somewhere else quite different from that action.

It is normal that our mind is constantly in movement, repeating frequently what we focus our attention on, what we have done lately and to which we have dedicated more time.

In it there is an incessant flow of information, so that emotions flourish without control, conditioning everything you do and resurrecting memories of the past; while you are still there, watching in silence, becoming a witness who does nothing to stop that mechanism that so often repeated becomes a loop of thoughts that appears and disappears consuming energy that you need to develop your potential.

It makes us move forward

Actually, thought is what makes us move forward, because thanks to it we go through this journey of life always looking for a way to expand and to be able to spread "what we are", expressing what is in our mind at every moment.

Because of thoughts we do not stop, we continue without stopping in that endless torrent of images that arise in our mind and that in most cases capture us, hindering us, imprisoning our attention and preventing us from observing clearly what is really beyond, in that other space where everything freezes, where our "true self" rests and obstacles and difficulties disappear; that inner space where everything stops and you find yourself.

Sometimes, thoughts also immobilize you, because they contain ideas that suspend your will, that imprison you in an endless loop where you feel caged by being trapped in an accumulation of toxic thoughts that trap you unconsciously.

The thoughts are formed without you hardly realizing it; it is a flow of images that were recorded in the deepest part of your memory and that occupy a space in your mind and come to dominate much of your will in an automatic way.

If you are in silence and in a situation of inner calm, you can observe this whole process that develops at great speed and that in reality is what makes you act in most cases.

Everything resides in that space where some thoughts are associated with others, where your intentions are consolidated and what you want to do is reinforced until the moment arrives when you decide to put it into practice. Everything starts there, in that lively place where thoughts concur while you just accept them without further ado.

In reality, they are the ones that direct you, the ones that set you on a certain path.

The thought invades our mind in a growing process, making changes in our state of mind. It arises spontaneously, wasting energy and disturbing our tranquility.

There are thoughts that confuse us, that cause us disorder and lead us to enhance our imagination in such a way that it becomes an inexhaustible source of harmful fantasies that last in time.

Sometimes, they can provoke chaos in you, making you live in an apparent, imaginary reality, enveloping you in a deep fiction that gradually ties you up in a transitory illusion that slowly takes away your reason.

When it comes to negative thoughts, everything around us is annulled; they burst with force into our mind causing us a disorder that captures all our attention and removes our own inner peace, which only manifests itself when we do not let ourselves be absorbed by all those images in the form of mental contents that are recreated in our consciousness, causing us an impulsive stimulation.

Everything that causes you affliction, in reality are thoughts that are spreading through your mind. When you contemplate them, you feel that little by little they ignite an emotion in you that leads you to discouragement, to feel that there exists in the deepest part of yourself a discord that is necessary to dominate in order to stop living in this unpleasant situation.

In fact, everything that goes through your mind alters you in some way, producing changes in you that sometimes can cause you nervousness, anguish, or make you live in an illusion that only exists in your own imagination.

Faced with this, your mood changes without resistance, reacting to each content, to each trace left in
your consciousness by all those elements that follow
one after the other, grouping together and concentrat-
ing all your attention.

In many occasions, you just follow them, enclosed
in your mind, living in the illusion that this spring of
thoughts is creating inside you.

What we think is not who we are

Thanks to the use of our consciousness, we can establish a difference between what we think constantly,
in a repetitive way, and what we really are, which is
something that is separate from our own thought,
from all those contents that arise from our memory
simply because we have stored them there, through
our contact with the world and thanks to the experiences we have had over time.

Sometimes what we think does not correspond to
what we are. The content of our own thoughts, many
times, has nothing to do with what we really want to
be, because it obeys to a kind of material that we have
been assimilating coming from the outside, that has
come to us from outside and does not resemble what
we really want to be, all those things that we really
want to do to continue feeling ourselves at all times.

Thanks to the observation that we can exercise on
our own mind, we will be more and more aware of this
difference. Not everything you think has to do with
who you are, with what you would really like to do.
Many of your thoughts that arise unexpectedly in your
consciousness do so because they obey the way in

which you have built your mental structure, the way in which you have elaborated your own ideas about the world and about yourself.

That is why it is necessary to establish this separation, between what your own thought proposes to you at every moment and what you really are.

Only if we reach a high level of observation of ourselves, we can realize this difference between these two areas: between our mind and what we are, which is beyond our own ideas and everything that has come to us from outside and that does not belong to our "true essence", it is not part of the being that we are.

PROGRAMMING

Representations come to one's mind: images accompanied by emotions that cause an effect and an agitation that remain imprinted in us. Each evocation that arises in our consciousness has an impact and leaves an imprint in the form of a memory, it is engraved like a stamp leaving a trail in the memory.

In this way, each movement that flows in our mind, each oscillation in the form of activity, generates a course of sensations that take hold of us; reaching our own will, which in many occasions remains immobile, stagnant, subject in that thought that stops and stills us, that is redoubled and reiterated in time; that we follow without limitations, prolonging it in actions that we repeat over and over again, always repeating the same issues, with no other objective than to maintain the same scheme of contents that we have always had embedded in the deepest part of ourselves.

It is a programming that we have implanted in ourselves, always reiterating the same ideas, continuously reproducing the same contents, which are duplicated with new premises, thanks to our capacity to add new arguments to the same subject, constantly.

When this happens, numerous thoughts circulate at great speed generating a current in us that leads us to repeated actions, and to spend our energy through uncontrolled impulses that make us enter a continuous, spontaneous loop, where we flow pouring all our strength in a river of perennial habits.

Over time we get used to that usual whirlwind, so that we start repeating it constantly, until we turn it into a chronic, daily programming, which spreads through every corner of our mind making us repeat the same action continuously.

We cannot let ourselves be carried away by the thought, since this in most of the occasions is presented to us in a disorganized way: it appears impulsively in a mechanical way in our mind by mere habit, by the habit of always thinking about the same contents, provoking us to execute an action if we look at them, if we obey everything that they propose to us.

We cannot be guided by all that which suddenly appears in our mind, since a great part of those elements that appear in our conscience have not been previously analyzed, we have not stopped to make that necessary pause to observe their content, the consequences of following certain approaches and acting according to those ideas without having stopped at least for an instant on them.

AFFIRMATIONS

We allow ourselves to be captured by everything that happens in our mind, by all those affirmations that seduce us and that consolidate a series of contents to which we grant relevance; in such a way that they come to manifest themselves more frequently.

That to which we give continuity extends repeatedly and expands within us gradually; thus establishing thought structures that over time are difficult to eliminate, since they remain imprinted in such a way that it is very difficult to extinguish them.

We must pay special attention to all those affirmations that we express about ourselves, because they tend to appear again and again, and if they are negative, they will contribute to create an idea of what we are that we will keep for a long time.

If they do not coincide with the truth, we will have inaccurate beliefs about ourselves, which will be retained in our deepest memory and will become permanent over time.

We may not see in a clear way the origin of all those components that flow in our mind and that separate us from what we are; they are contents that are hidden in our memory and that in many occasions are reborn relieving other kind of thoughts, in such a way that they are suggesting us little by little, adding elements of our own imagination that in the end are delimiting and conditioning us, because finally they lead us to walk through a path full of doubts that little by little are overwhelming us, separating us from ourselves.

HIDDEN CONTENTS

When you do not force your mind, it becomes creative, other contents arise in it that are normally kept hidden, because they are somewhat separated from the usual thoughts.

When your mind calms down, thanks to inner calm, these other more withdrawn thoughts come to light. Then you perceive internally a series of deeper contents; unlike the usual ones which are somewhat more superficial.

Thanks to these other thoughts that have more to do with yourself, you can discover many things about yourself that you did not know; they take you away somehow from that superficial image that you can create in contact with the outside, in the relationship with others; they are deeper and less usual thoughts that connect you with what you really are.

These kinds of thoughts, which provide you with a more objective vision of yourself, can only be accessed if we reach a state of stillness where inner peace reigns in us, which slows everything down and provides you with a space in which you can observe yourself and pay attention to other kinds of contents that have more to do with your own inner world than with the world outside: with all those visible circumstances that usually surround you.

They provide you with a knowledge that helps you later in everything you do in your life. This self-knowledge guides you along the path that best suits what you really want to be, what you really want to achieve. It is related to what is your "inner purpose": with the true path that you think you have to follow in

order to act always in accordance with what you really
are, deep inside yourself.

Habitual thoughts, on the other hand, are more
linked to the material world, to what we do on the outside or to our own habits that we constantly repeat.

9. Imagination

When we perceive inwardly what is in our consciousness, which are nothing more than thoughts and ideas that are there for the purpose of leading us to concrete action, we observe our judgments in a more reflective, more considered way.

The fact of being able to examine, even briefly, that process that occurs in our mind, in that part of the consciousness where reflections and concepts are formed, makes our reason find a more precise explanation to all that we judge, to all that we frequently think.

It is only necessary to observe those images that wander through our mind and that form structures of thought that make us think and deduce, sometimes wrongly, what we should believe; what we have to consider true and what not; what we can imagine; the rest of things that can be left aside because they cannot be understood: to which we have not yet found a logical explanation; to everything that piles up in our memory without knowing its origin and its reason for being.

It is about discovering how this process works, through which we set an idea in motion, and from a few brief reflections, thanks to our imaginative capacity, sometimes we begin to invent an illusion that can make us live in fiction for a certain time, under the whims of a delirium, a mirage or a utopia.

All that happens, when we leave our ingenuity to its free will, has to do with our capacity for invention, with the way we use our sharpness to create new judgments that make us understand the reasons: those causes that explain the reasons behind those problems that we do not understand, that we do not know how to solve because we lack arguments; premises to find a convincing clarification, an interpretation that solves our doubts; conclusions that remedy that which we do not know how to decipher.

You can imagine other worlds

All your mental content spills unceremoniously into your own interior, so that it takes over your imagination, which takes care of making a world according to your desires, which sometimes coincides with what you are, but sometimes not.

Every idea that enters your consciousness awakens your interest in some way. Sometimes you dig into some more than others, depending on the degree of attraction they have on you. In the event that they allude to a content that really captivates you, they can remain there almost inexhaustibly.

Thoughts have the faculty to move you to another place, so you can imagine other worlds to try to free yourself from the anguish you may be suffering in this one.

Your mind has the capacity to perceive another reality, more extraordinary and amazing than the one that may be happening in front of you. It can appear to occupy your entire consciousness, while you limit yourself to observing and examining all that is hidden in that illusory world that can openly deceive you with a set of uncertain fantasies.

Both worlds, real and imaginary, can coexist. You can live in one while the other slowly diffuses inside you, captivating you little by little, in a process where you abandon some thoughts and hide them in oblivion.

There are moments when you may feel confused, when you try to move from one world to another. You understand that there is no harmony, that you are only obeying impulses that are driving you in an unappealable way.

You feel that your behaviors are linked to thought structures in an automatic way, so that everything that passes through your mind becomes an action, without being able to make a serious judgment that leads you to understand the purpose of everything you do.

When you live in a world created by your own imagination, you feel indifferent to the reality that surrounds you, separated from external circumstances. You are more aware of that which originates in your mind than of observing exactly that which surrounds you, every situation that blossoms before you.

In this way your mind becomes a set of manifestations that isolate you from the real world, where you have to solve the difficulties that it poses in each circumstance.

This ability to invent other parallel worlds within ourselves, has its explanation and is based on the need to flee from reality itself, out of fear or because we do not know how to solve the various difficulties that we find in it.

In our particular world of illusion we can invent a new existence, far from external circumstances, which is only visible to us, because it will be elaborated with our peculiar way of understanding the world and everything that has happened to us before. It will be a new reality adapted to our own needs; although in some aspects it may coincide with what we find outside.

Many times we let ourselves be carried away by our imagination, by any image or idea that in those moments clouds our thoughts and makes us suppose that there is something beyond the truths that surround us.

And it is that, in many occasions, we tend to maintain for long periods of time an endless number of fantasies that we conceive trying to avoid reality, when it does not happen as we wish or simply because it does not happen in the way we had foreseen.

In those moments, we resort to the power of our ingenuity to devise an invention: an illusion that at least satisfies us for a certain time, until we realize that it is only a reverie that we invented to deny the truth and the state of our own existence.

With time we discover the chimeras and mirages with which we often feed our fiction: our delusions, which lead us to a vision of the world closer to hallucination than to reality itself, which day after day sprouts in the space where we live and which makes us see the certainty of life: what we finally are, what we have been before, and what we are going to be afterwards.

If these kinds of contents remain too long in your mind, they somehow get stronger, and later it becomes more difficult to mitigate them. If you allow it, this kind of thoughts can flood everything, they can drown you in a world of false illusions, making you live in a fiction that occupies your whole mind, leading you to imagine implausible things that can extend in time inexorably.

It is easy for us to imagine a non-existent reality, and also a way of seeing ourselves very different from what we really are. All this is due to a deformation on our part when analyzing the information that comes to us from outside, as well as all those contents that are manifested in our thoughts, when we draw erroneous conclusions; when we imagine or suppose through false beliefs, irrational thoughts that do not explain accurately how things really are.

We can invent deceptions

In your imagination your thoughts are transformed and somehow the truth is distorted. You establish connections of ideas that at times become confused with reality itself. So you can arrive at statements that you have never thought of before; you can draw wrong conclusions that reinforce your beliefs about what you are or about life in general.

From all that is created in our consciousness, we can invent deceptions and any fiction, which can alter the order of things; they can even change us if we deceive the truth by adulterating what we are seeing, both outside and inside ourselves.

Sometimes, our intelligence uses our capacity of reasoning to create ideas about ourselves that in many occasions are not exact, they lack objectivity; they belong rather to the world of fiction.

All this leads us to deception, it leads us to believe what we are not, because we let ourselves be guided by those erroneous thoughts that we have invented to conceive a different life, far from suffering and the truth of daily facts, which follow one after the other undressing us, uncovering our true nature, our mistakes and all those limitations that prevent us from getting where we really want to be.

We should not believe many of the judgments we make, because in many cases they are just mere opinions without a solid explanation, with a reasoned analysis that leads us to those conclusions. The bad thing is that all that we think about ourselves, we come to believe and accept without further ado.

We must learn to distrust what we take for valid without first having demonstrated it, without having a reason that certifies and accredits that these assessments, which we sometimes make, are justified and based on evidence.

We are required to observe

To realize that this happens, we need to look, in a more detailed way, at everything we believe in: what we judge without suspecting that we may be wrong, those things we take for granted, without considering that there may be other variants, more alternatives within the same option.

It is enough to contemplate all that happens in our consciousness, to realize that there is another reality within ourselves, which has its own existence and is in action permanently, through a whole accumulation of incessant thoughts that move repeatedly without us being able to exercise control over them, unless we are awake, unless we make an act of presence in this universe of perennial images that cling to us constantly.

This mechanism resides in us and sometimes it is inevitable that it works that way, but thanks to our observation capacity we become aware of this process, we can become aware of how all those thoughts that inhabit our imagination are unified and that sometimes form a vision of life closer to madness than to reality itself.

Calm is recommended

For this series of situations it is also recommended the use of calm, of that soft stillness that little by little is reproduced in your world orienting correctly all those thoughts that are accumulating in your conscience and that openly are more proper of the imagination than of the own reality.

Thanks to our imagination we can be in another place, with thoughts other than those required to perform a particular activity. It is what our own mind allows us, the way in which we are designed; so the ability to be able to pause in all that constant thought has to be learned through practice, since it does not come naturally to us.

10. Self-control

Sometimes we obey a thought as if we were submitting to it, as if we were allowing ourselves to be controlled without stopping to examine its origin; we simply allow ourselves to be governed by allowing it to direct us, to lead us towards a certain action.

We allow ourselves to be transported, in a way, because it is thought that guides us in the way we act. In this way we come to elaborate patterns of behavior allowing ourselves to be led by an idea, with hardly any participation on our part, without having too much influence.

We simply limit ourselves to execute a series of actions that make us function in a way that in many occasions is not governed by our own will, by what we would really like to do.

It is a way of acting without intervening, allowing ourselves to be led, allowing other processes to manage our way of directing ourselves, the way we orient ourselves through life, to direct our actions and to consciously manage everything that happens around us.

We allow our thoughts to rule over us, to manipulate us, to operate in a certain way, leading us to proceed in an unconscious way, often involuntarily.

When this happens, we simply abstain, we allow our behavior to work and work in an involuntary way; it is as if we were going through life without having control over what we do, as if we were moving as if we were absent and far away from what we are, since in that march, in that path, we do not command in a conscious way, we do not walk by ourselves walking the path that we really want to walk; And all because we let our own mind be responsible for our movements, we allow it to be the one that takes us and transports us in every trip we make, every time we run absent, without hardly stopping to recognize that we are not the ones who decide our way of walking.

You can take the lead

With mindfulness focused on what circulates in your mind, you get to place yourself at another level of consciousness from which you can control the meaning and direction of your own thoughts; In this case, all that flow of contents and images that arise automatically, in this case, is done in a controlled way, since you are the one who in that moment takes control of that space, so that everything that arises does not do it automatically, but is the result of a deliberate decision, that starts from the control and from what you want to happen in each moment; from what you are looking for to give meaning to what you observe in that moment within your consciousness.

In these cases, everything that occurs in your mind is under your control, under the protection of what you want to create through your imagination and the combination of all those thoughts that you decide and that have some relation with each other, with some matter that at that moment may interest you and that you want to pay attention to, because you consider it necessary for you.

It is you, in such a case, the one who takes the control and decides and selects what happens in your mind, thanks to this observing capacity that is reached through practice, in moments of stillness and silence where nothing can distract you.

You can analyze everything in a more leisurely way, from that posture in which you are the one who exercises control over each mental content that arises from the depths of your memory, which becomes visible and of which you are aware at all times, which you can vary and eliminate as you see fit; so that it does not exert on you any kind of power and influence that takes you away from that state of control.

You are the one who, in some way, consents to each content that causes you suffering. And it is that everything originates from that instant where a thought manifests itself in your consciousness and at the same time ignites others that finally end up taking over your mind.

Only through the contest of our will, we can make great progress towards the mastery of our own mind.

It makes you have a greater control over yourself and you become the master of your own thoughts; you can even govern your own emotions derived from them. You manage to take control of everything that happens inside you, so that you can find yourself in a privileged position that isolates you from any influence, both external and internal.

When you take the reins of your mind, you take the reins of your own life. From then on, everything starts to be different. The change is quite considerable, the one you can experience when you manage to dominate your thoughts and your attention is only focused on what really matters.

Thanks to this you can exercise greater control - establish a distance over everything that can distract you and take you away from that path-, and continue on that path of silence and inner peace that leads you to find yourself, in the depths of your being; that makes you know yourself as you really are, in a place where time does not exist and you are the one who dominates that space where the forms and mental objects from your memory appear.

With time you will feel that this control will become greater and greater, that little by little you will take control of everything that happens in your inner world, reaching great discoveries about what you really are.

To conquer our mind is to dominate ourselves, it is to control everything that happens to us internally.

Through observation

Through the personal effort of slow observation, through meditation, we can achieve great achievements in terms of mastery of our own thoughts, of that constant activity that takes place in our own mind and in which we are not aware, since we barely stop to observe what happens within ourselves, which makes us behave in a certain way: repeating habits continuously that we can not stop; although many times we try and we strive to eliminate them completely.

When you connect with yourself in that inner space away from thought, you enter another deeper dimension from which you can observe yourself, contemplating everything that happens inside you.

At that moment you gain control of your inner world, so that you can decide the kind of contents that will circulate in your consciousness and to which you want to pay attention.

Generally, thoughts impose themselves on you, so that you are executing them without being very conscious of it. Sometimes, they incapacitate you to see reality as it is; in such a way that they lead you to a confusion that clouds your ideas and everything that may arise in those moments of your memory.

In order to detach yourself from this process, which can absorb you without you realizing it, you only need to observe how these contents are reproduced and how they are formed trying to force you to act. If you do not let yourself be guided by them, they will not fulfill their purpose, so they will gradually cease and become weaker and weaker, so that they will lose all their power and begin to slowly dismantle from your consciousness.

The strength of thought weakens when it is examined; when you discover what is hidden behind each image that you observe in your consciousness; when you are able to stop and capture all that content that arises in your mind and do not let yourself be seduced by any impulse; when you just limit yourself to remain still, serene, without moving away from your center: from that space away from adversity where all confusion disappears and you feel isolated from the noise and any influence that may appear, and that tries to separate you from that fertile place that is your inner world.

Until we are able to dominate the space occupied by those thoughts, which so often stun us, we cannot penetrate into that other dimension that exists within ourselves, where we can examine everything from another position, if we remain in a situation of stillness and carefully observe everything that is hidden inside, which often leads us to bitterness and accumulate anguish that is gradually knocking us down and separating us from what we really are.

Any thought can take hold of us, altering the mental order, making us live in an imbalance that can affect our own existence.

The fact that they are repeated over and over again makes them grow stronger, so that they do not dissolve until you are not aware that this is happening.

If you contemplate them, from a distance, without taking any action, then they begin to lose momentum, they gradually become shorter and shorter, so that they become quiet until they become neutral, harmless, and are slowly eliminated from your consciousness.

If we submit ourselves to our own thoughts, we run the risk of living in an uncertain life, so it is necessary to have some time to have the opportunity to examine them (that would be advisable); not to let ourselves be absorbed by all those mental objects that take over our imagination leading us to a sense of unhappiness that tenaciously extinguishes any clarity.

It is the best way to reach that source of wisdom that is in you, in your own inner self, but that does not bloom until you clear your mind of all those toxic contents that cloud your understanding and your reason for being. In this way you can redirect your ideas, everything you think about a particular issue that at a given time may be causing you suffering.

It is a way to stop those automatic thoughts that flood us uncontrollably, that take over our will without us being aware of it.

It is a way to get control of your own thinking, which can help you to redirect all those behaviors that then become habits, that take you away from what you really want to do. If you do not master this process, in the end you end up repeating a series of automatic behaviors, without any control, leading to the creation of patterns of behavior that will become part of what is your mental programming.

Through calmness

The only way to temper the energy of all these compulsive thoughts that often lead you to confusion is by resorting to stillness. Only from there can you transform the course of all that mental noise into a silence that will gradually take you away from those thoughts and will spread in you an inner peace that will invite you to find yourself; in that space where everything is suspended, where the mind dissolves and the appearance of each thought is progressively prolonged in time, filling that surface with a silent emptiness, far from memory and imagination itself.

If we look for moments of silence, these can help us to intervene on the frequency in which thoughts appear, so that we can lengthen in time those spaces between one thought and another, keeping a greater and greater distance between them.

We can do this if we completely isolate ourselves from external distractions, which can break those moments of stillness and make us return to our usual way of functioning.

You can achieve this when you enter a state of inner calm, of serene peace, which is only possible in a situation of silence in which you can observe yourself.

In such a situation, you encounter no obstacles, no impediments. All the difficulties suddenly begin to evaporate through the immensity of your mind, which leads you to a strange abandonment, where little by little you are detaching yourself from what you do not need, while in your whole being spreads a temperate inner peace that little by little is moving away from that surface that is your confused mind.

When this happens and you reach this privileged situation, you can organize yourself a little better inside. You have the possibility to select what suits you best and put aside all those toxic elements that often haunt your head and take you away from your "true purpose", forcing you to perform behaviors that eventually become unwanted habits that are perpetuated over time.

And the fact is that, thanks to calmness, sometimes, we manage to dissipate all that mental exaltation that sometimes spreads through our own mind, which is imported from our unconscious through a series of contents that suddenly make their way and occupy our consciousness, without giving us a break to move them elsewhere.

They can be reproduced over and over again in an unequivocal way; nothing can extinguish them except silence. A silence that focuses on separating you from the noise of the mind, that separates you from all those contents that take you away from what you are, from your own being; from that space where the truth can be glimpsed, where you feel free, because there you will not find anything that has the capacity to affect you, to dissuade you or to lead you to discouragement.

If there is no calmness we cannot face everything that the mind proposes to us; we cannot embrace that inner peace that fixes everything, that leads us to a harmony that separates us from suffering and pacifies anxiety, creating an inner atmosphere where we discover the being that we are, and we come to understand all those confusions that from time to time stun us, taking us to the limit.

Thanks to the inner stillness we find certainties, that which makes us escape from the darkness and provides us with an individual freedom that makes us live away from judgments and all those labels that we often put quickly to any circumstance we live.

Somehow, it is a way to control your own thought, which always tries to force you to perform an action, even if you are not very conscious; although for this you have your own will to decide whether to do it or not, when you are in a situation in which you can freely choose the option you most want at that moment; but that can only happen if you are in a position in which you have control of that process, by observing all this that happens inside your own mind.

You will see that no thought, in that situation, can influence you; nothing that comes from your mind can affect you, when you take control of that area, in which you are alone with yourself and you are in control of everything that happens in that inner, hidden world, which is in another dimension, in that part of your consciousness in which you are with yourself, away from your habitual thoughts and all those external influences that constantly overwhelm you.

All this gives you the possibility to order, in a more exhaustive way, your own ideas: all those chaotic thoughts that often flood you and make you confused when interpreting reality, which you observe both outside and inside yourself.

If we let ourselves be carried away by the mind and by everything that it is proposing at every moment, it is easy for chaos to take hold of you and for you to find enormous difficulty in finding the truth of things; when it comes to assessing everything that is happening in your life in its proper measure.

All the noise and toxic thoughts will be eliminated. Your mind will cease to be irrational; it will cease to be that prison that makes you live in a mechanical, robotic world, in which you barely have time to be yourself, because all that makes you move in a continuous circle that forces you to live in the past, or pending the future, with no other purpose than to remain active and always in the same direction.

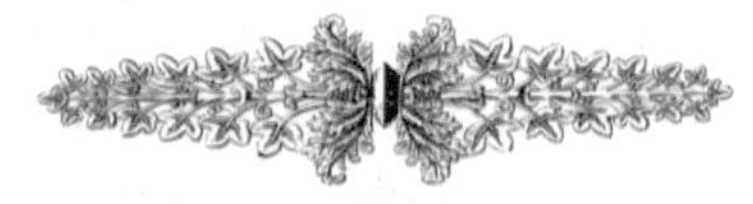

11. Action

That which is reproduced in your mind is what guides you throughout your life. It is the product of an accumulation of contents coming from your experience that are lodged in your memory. They arise in your mind almost automatically, without you being very conscious of it, and they take over your consciousness, guiding your thoughts in a specific direction, towards a specific theme.

In fact, this process is what leads us to act, to carry out a series of actions related to those contents that previously arise in our mind and that catch us in such a way that they capture all our attention and lead us to the realization of a concrete activity.

In our inner world we fabricate our way of acting, which in reality depends on the contents of our own thoughts, which appear in our consciousness, most of the time, in a redundant way, forcing us to move along a path that many times we do not want, that does not have much to do with what we really long for.

We cannot stop to reflect, to fix our attention on any idea that crosses our mind. Our intelligence makes us dig constantly, paying attention to everything that arises in our consciousness, whether it has a purpose or not.

The fact is that our mind always suggests a proposal, something that we have to decide on. So that idea that we think we end up developing it, we submit it to an action that in the end, after many repetitions, we turn it into an activity that together with others, shapes our life.

In reality, our existence is made up of small actions that allow us to have a movement where we consume our energy, where we invest our time. These actions shape, in a way, what we end up being; they adjust our character and many other attributes among which are our will, temperament and the spirit with which we do things.

According to the nature of our actions, we will distinguish our own identity, since these are the distinctive, our way of expressing ourselves outwardly and the means by which other people can know us.

Everything we do reflects our way of being, the firmness with which we do it and all those qualities that make up our aptitude, disposition and personal conditions to perform a specific task.

Our talent is also reflected in what we do; our training and the system we use to solve the different difficulties that arise; the discipline and habits we have when we perform certain actions, many of which become habits through repetitive practice.

Everything we repeat becomes a routine, so that we learn to always use the same procedure, the same method, as if it were a repetitive rite, when executing a behavior or following the guidelines we are accustomed to.

If we look at it, most of the time we perform the same actions, through frequent acts that keep us busy repeating always the same operations. We do not stop, even for a single moment, to observe our own behavior, which actually originates in our mind through a thought that arises in our consciousness from the data we have stored from the past.

This actually limits us, it leads us to have a mind-dependent attitude, so that we allow ourselves to be dragged and act in communion with whatever we think at any given moment, depending on the circumstances.

Therefore, we could say that our life, at times, is conditioned by our own mind; and it is something that we cannot easily change, since at all times we feel the need to act and we are not always able to stop and stop behaving like a robot, to strive to have a conscious attitude, walking the path more in line with our true purpose; in this way there would be no dilemma within us.

Because we live in an unconscious way, without discovering our full potential, which is hidden in that other, deeper dimension that lies within ourselves; in that other part of the mind where we are conscious and do not let ourselves be carried away by thought and by that mental activity that often traps us and conditions us in such a way that in the end we end up converting every thought into behavior and actions.

Reinforcement

One always has illusions: those sensations that are appreciated when you see that your intention is fulfilled, that in the end it becomes a reality; that what in the beginning was just a desire, takes on a life of its own, becomes something that you can see, verify that it has happened, even if you did not have much hope at the beginning.

And the fact is that when something that was only in our mind takes shape, becomes action, something we can recognize, it gains a lot of power, so that it impacts on us leaving a constant impression, that does not fade with the passage of time; it does not vanish from our memory so easily.

It remains there, all-encompassing, penetrating deep within us, so that it captures all our attention for a prolonged period of time; it grips us in such a way that we think only of that subject. We cannot prevent it from enveloping us and obscuring other thoughts and other ideas that may also be of interest to us at a given moment.

When this happens, we become totally involved in that which has a result for us, in that which has consequences, the desired effects. Depending on the fruit and the performance that we observe in that which we are trying hardest, so will be our involvement, our subsequent intervention.

If we understand that there is a positive outcome, fruitful for us, we will continue to maintain a submission, a submission to that idea, to that purpose; as long as it continues to give us enough profit to understand that it is useful, that it is important and that it is worthwhile to continue insisting on it, even if it entails adherence to a certain way of thinking or to reduce us to act in a defined, concrete way.

We only decide to repeat actions that have a specific effect, so that if we repeat an activity in which we do not obtain any benefit or utility, we finally put it aside, because we do not see the fruit to obtain sufficient re-inforcement to continue to maintain it over time.

Everything we do is a consequence of previous performance, of the positive effect it has previously had on us. Through our experience we are verifying the things that really are of benefit, all those issues to which we can get a benefit, even if it involves an effort on our part; we will be willing to do it if we get the outcome that we anticipate.

CONTROL

Sometimes, days turn into small moments where you barely have a chance to observe the events that are happening. In such circumstances, you become someone who is limited to developing a set pattern of behaviors that you have learned by dint of practice.

You carry out your performance by acting in a way that does not really satisfy you, since you are not really convinced of what you are doing.

Do not get carried away by impulses

The most advisable thing to do is not to let ourselves be guided by our most immediate impulses, since these obey a series of unconscious patterns that we are hardly aware of. We only witness the presence of these impulses when we end up executing an action and we see the results of this; then, sometimes, we stop to analyze what has provoked that reaction in us, that way of acting, what has driven us to proceed in a certain way.

We have the opportunity to observe the moment in which this has occurred, even if we are a little deeper, the reason that has originated that automatic impulse that has come upon us and that has led us to act in that particular way; in this way we can come to understand our behavior, often automatic and uncontrolled.

In this way we not only manage to understand it, but we also open a way, a door to be able to control it in the future; since being aware of this mechanism that is behind every act we perform, it is possible to reach a control of ourselves, especially of those habits with which we are not satisfied and that we would like to try to eliminate.

If we do not allow ourselves to be carried away by these impulses, we will have gained a great deal of ground against the influence that our mind exerts over us. It is only possible if we establish this separation between that which occurs in our mind, in the form of thought, and ourselves; if we separate the observed from the one who observes, from the one who witnesses what is happening.

To do this we must look in a distanced way, without anything influencing you, without that which you perceive leading you to be something other than what you are.

Observe what is happening

In us there is the faculty to observe this process, so that when we are aware of it, all those contents that occupy our mind cease to have influence on us, so that we can establish a distance with all those elements that we have the opportunity to observe. In these cases we achieve that a certain thought, no matter how intense it is, does not lead us to an action that we do not really want.

If we focus on our mind for a moment, we get to observe what is going on inside us. So we can choose the best option to act; in this way there is no conflict, because what we decide to do at that moment will always be the most appropriate, because we are deciding from that dimension in which we have the possibility to decide for ourselves and not unconsciously, as usual.

Any moment is propitious to become aware and conscious of what you are observing. It is enough to have a little will and to be aware of this process, knowing that at any moment you can establish a distance between what is around you and yourself. In this way you can reach a certain objectivity about what you see, about your own conclusions about what you perceive.

This distance that you can manage to maintain can also help you to achieve a control over yourself that is not possible to achieve if you keep acting in your usual way.

There are many stimuli that surround us, and it is normal that in the end we get carried away by what attracts our attention the most, by what has the greatest impact on us at a given moment. If we are aware and remember in those moments that this can happen, it can be a good starting point to curb, somehow, all those behaviors that you do not want but in the end you end up doing in an uncontrolled and unconscious way, forced by all those distractions around you and trying to catch you calling your attention.

When we reach this point, only if we establish this distance, we can control ourselves; nothing can affect us: neither the noise of our unconscious mind, nor the distractions coming from the external world in the form of stimuli, which try to distract us and separate us from that moment in which we are inside that space of consciousness where we take control of all those mental contents that appear disorganized and impulsively; and that lead us to act in many occasions without hardly having the will to be able to stop all that energy that comes from our own interior.

You will immediately realize each and every one of the habits that lead you to waste time, and what you have to do to change them.

This would be the way to reach the control of our own thoughts, through a slow observation of the process that occurs in our mind.

Control through calmness

To reach this state of observation requires that you find yourself, at the same time, in a situation of internal calm that keeps you away from any distraction of the external world and also from all that mental noise that somehow also distances you from that state of observation that has to be achieved so that everything that happens in your mind stops affecting you.

Once you get to this point, you can achieve your own self-control. To the extent that you gain control of what is happening inside you, you can at the same time put some order in all those thoughts that assail you automatically, altering the mental order and leading you to a continuous confusion that prevents you from achieving the necessary balance to be conscious and think in a correct way.

The fact that your mind becomes calmer, makes everything work more slowly, so it is easier to control certain processes that usually work mechanically and are virtually impossible to stop. Thanks to your capacity of observation and this possibility of being aware of everything that happens, you can direct your own behavior where you really want it to go.

Remaining in a state of inner calm also brings you in control of your own behavior, because it allows you to have enough time to stop all those uncontrolled impulses that sometimes flood us and which we do not know how to stop.

If you get used to stay like this for long periods of time during the day, you can exercise control over most of your behaviors, thus bringing about a change in your most repetitive habits.

You can get to create a new mental programming, by incorporating new behaviors, thanks to the establishment of this pause that allows you to discriminate between the actions that are positive for you and those that are not; that allows you to put a stop to all those habits in which you waste your time and in which you lose all your energies without hardly realizing it.

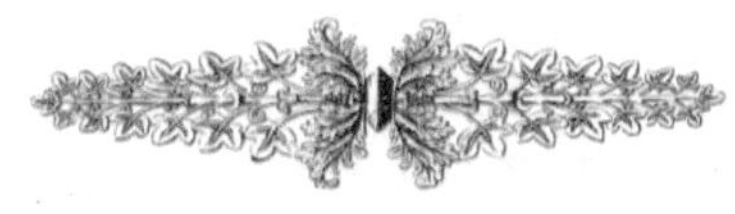

12. Experience

In the deepest part of ourselves, our thoughts, in the form of images, form ideas that make us have a conception of the world.

In fact, they create a mentality that is generated little by little with the passage of time, which reproduces all that content that we have incubated in our memory, coming from each and every one of the experiences we have lived over the years.

All those thoughts that are produced in our mind, are spreading all the matters and issues that we have had the opportunity to observe and perceive around us, in each and every one of the contexts where we have been before.

And the fact is that we all harbor in the depths of our memory, all that we have lived, which are the traces of our past, the impressions of all that we have contemplated before, even those things that we have treasured without realizing, without hardly realizing that they were before us, that we have observed without looking at them, without having had the opportunity to appreciate them in their right measure.

All those ideas we have of the world and of ourselves, are conceived in our own mind, through all the contents we have accumulated over time, through all our past experiences, which become relevant information that is stored in our memory and remains there, available for those moments when we need to find an explanation, an argument, to some issue we are trying to understand through our own reason.

Your experiences are recorded impressions, which in many occasions you awaken without realizing it, when your mind resorts to the past to interpret the present. It then delves into your memories, and through the mechanism of imagination resurrects what remains dormant.

They accumulate in your memory. When you feel you have problems, you turn to them to try to find a solution. You force your mind to look for a way out.

All your past experiences, acquired through contact with your external world, re-emerge back into your consciousness because they are planted as seeds in the depths of your memories.

They sleep in your mind like traces that are not dead, for they move about seeking to emerge again in the form of evocation in the present; they never disappear, for they constitute your past, your memory.

Utility

All that information remains within us, it will be useful to indicate us the way to proceed; the way to execute a determined action, even without having carried it out previously. All the data accumulated in our memory will help us to carry out what we propose, if we know how to use them conveniently at the time of carrying out that activity.

Experience is always a lesson for us, a teaching by which we learn a whole class of contents that we accumulate over time. Everything we learn occupies a position in our memory, it is placed there occupying a rank, depending on the meaning it has for us, according to the circumstances and conditions in which we have obtained that information.

All the contents that we have been assimilating will remain in that situation, occupying a state of waiting, in a scenario in which it is possible that they will resurface to our consciousness at any moment, when some question related to those contents comes to our mind. In that case we will seek to give a meaning to those impressions that at that moment we have in our consciousness; and for that we will look for, within the traces of our memory, the appropriate concepts to give meaning and relevance to that which at that moment has an interest for us.

In many occasions it happens that this information that we already have, is wasted, it is not used in the most adequate way. It all depends on where we put our focus of attention when performing a particular task. If we focus all our interest only on what we do in each moment, if we deploy all our faculties in developing our best skills in the performance of what we do every day, we will be taking advantage of the best of our experiences, of what we have been assimilating, little by little, of each lesson that life has been teaching us.

When you meditate, you can observe them and ask yourself why they remain there and why they condition your decisions, because they are forgotten realities that have already occurred and that simply remain there, stored, right at the door of your consciousness, which in most cases resorts to the past to project its thoughts in a mechanical way.

You are your teacher

The teaching of life is a lesson that is not learned in any school, it is an apprenticeship that guides you in those things you need to know. The experience is forming you throughout the time, giving you a training that prepares you to face the different difficulties that arise throughout your existence.

Life is nothing more than an apprenticeship where you are your own trainer, your teacher and the one who manages your own training about yourself. You are the supervisor and the responsible for everything that happens to you, so you should always have the control to follow and review everything that influences you and that in the end ends up affecting you for not knowing how to make a previous analysis checking the scope of each new experience you live.

You are the pilot who has to verify and follow up on what you observe and what is in front of you, because you must control all those important aspects that are part of the reality that surrounds you. You are the one who has to take into account the most important components, the factors that contribute to the fact that an event has certain consequences.

Depending on how well you do this task, your performance in life will be an enriching function, because your actions will always find harmony and meaning in all their manifestations.

Your activities will be the living image of coherence, since they will express in each of your interventions your commitment to what you are involved in at any given moment.

13. Suffering

Everything that oppresses us is created in our own mind; it is in charge of altering the order of our thoughts, preventing us from observing clearly and using our ingenuity in the best possible way.

We are constantly exposed to everything that is represented in our mind and that at a given moment can break our balance, with a whole series of contents that are associated with each other and lead us to an absorbing deception that assaults us, to the point that we come to form beliefs that condemn us to live in an illusion without results, without a minimum evidence that serves us to understand that we are on the true path.

We are not aware that, in most cases, it is we ourselves who seek our own torture, emphasizing only that which afflicts us, focusing our attention on all those stories of the past in which we suffered and experienced misfortune; on those moments of distress that tormented us.

We often try to dig into the wound, perhaps to see if we are able to tolerate suffering again. It is a way of testing ourselves, to see if we can break the vicious circle that once overwhelmed us; to see if we manage, at least for once, to rise above that which weakens us, that which makes us faint and consumes us; it is a way of sinking consciously into chaos.

And sometimes we are attracted to the shipwreck; to know what it feels like when everything falls apart, even for an instant. There are those who live in this permanent downfall, trying to throw their lives overboard. As they hide in a total sinking, they begin to be aware of the truth and of their own existence; although sometimes it is already too late to start living in the certainty of life.

Painful experiences

Some experiences are painful, so they can cause you grief, when you become aware of what hurt you and you keep thinking about it, even though years go by. You never manage to forget completely what once caused you an emotional wound. It still exists in your mind thanks to the memories, which in some way are the testimony of what happened and are what make you evoke the problems of the past.

In those moments you begin to experience the same emotions you felt when these experiences first occurred. When these memories flow through your consciousness there is no way to stop them, you just have to limit yourself to understand that you function this way and that your mind is using its own mechanisms, so the only thing you can do is to become, through meditation, an observer of what appears in your mind; whether they are memories of past failures or fantasies that you hope will be fulfilled in the future.

It is the only way to be conscious without being asleep; in this way all the contents will pass without affecting you, wherever they come from. It is the only way for suffering to be carried away by the wind, whether it is in the past or comes from the future.

This is how the mind works, and this can be a good technique to control it in some way, because in it there is always a movement, it is not easy for it to remain static -it is always alive in some way-; but if you know how to look inside and you realize what is happening there, you will immediately understand that the problems are nothing more than thoughts that arise from the past or are related to the future; that in these cases they are destructive and are reborn again and again from the bottom of your memory, although you may think that some of them are already dead.

In reality, they are engraved in each of the wounds of past experiences, and when they surface again, they confuse you again just as they did the first time, in an irrational way, while you lost your calm trying to interpret what was happening.

Do not strive to eliminate the experiences of the past, even if they seem dead, they will always remain there, waiting to become thoughts again. Limit yourself only to knowing yourself; to observe your consciousness, seeing how the images that emerge from your memory move through it, in order to keep yourself awake and not let yourself be carried away by the traces of your own memories.

Confusion

Sometimes, confusion rushes into your mind, it mixes with judgments that propitiate another reality very different from the usual one: the one you are used to.

This can be due to some contents that move without any foundation and that form beliefs that are established and remain imprinted in your mind, lacking all logic; which can produce an excessive torment in which you can not find a way to end these perpetual thoughts that unhinge you and that lead you to believe in statements that are only manufactured in your conscience and that you have not yet proven in real life.

And the fact is that, sometimes, a force spreads within us that takes us in an uncertain direction. This happens when we allow all those thoughts and beliefs that lead us to disorder to impose themselves and remain hidden in our memory waiting for an impulse to insert them back into consciousness.

Once they occupy all our mental space, they hit us little by little through judgments that entangle us in a confusion from which we cannot get out. They take over and lead us unexpectedly along paths that lead us to mental blockage and to a situation of restlessness that creates a dark disorder.

Some mental contents lead us to chaos, they stay for a long time in our mind and take over us making us change our vision of everything that happens around us.

You may find that your mind is apt to remain for a long time in a singular confusion, that it starts to filter thoughts that quickly change sense, imported from your memory, that manifest themselves without any difficulty running through your consciousness without you being able to eliminate them.

You may find some difficulty in following some mental elements, for some components enter into contradiction. On the one hand, they express themselves in terms that go in one direction, and soon after they begin to reveal the opposite.

And sometimes our judgments do not follow any criteria, they move away from prudence and moderation, they stun us with reasons that have no logic, separating us from sanity.

Sometimes your mind deceives you, because it hides the truth and leads you to chaos, leading you down uncertain paths that rob you of your understanding, creating thoughts that lead you to unhappiness, because they are irrational.

You can become a victim of your own self-deception, when you accept any thought that appears in your consciousness and let yourself be carried away by any impulse that disturbs and stirs your peace.

If you are guided by them, you will end up with a faulty conception of the world, for your thoughts, though inexhaustible, will always be incomplete.

FRUSTRATION

It is the intention that counts, the soul you put into it when you do something. There are times when your whole existence revolves around a particular issue, so that all your actions operate in the same direction.

You draw strength from where there is none to reach a goal that has been on your mind for a long time, creating an obsessive desire that has no end until you fulfill that purpose.

Sometimes, destiny and following the course of a good direction on your part, make you reach the end of the journey with the expected success, so you get the reward of knowing that the journey has been worthwhile.

On other occasions, when you do not achieve the expected goal, you understand that the expectations you set before starting that journey have not been fulfilled, so you are left with a feeling of having made a journey that has not been worthwhile, because you have not seen fulfilled the purpose you set before starting that adventure that you were so passionate about and in which you hoped that all your dreams would be fulfilled.

Although the risks were many, you thought that you would come up with something to solve the sets and all those kinds of incidents that could occur in an enterprise of this nature.

The fact is that, sometimes, an accumulation of circumstances can lead you to the most absolute failure, without anyone having previously advised you and without being trained to straighten the course towards other paths with more possibilities of success.

The problem arises when failure appears and we are flooded with frustration. We are not always prepared to face the setback that occurs when we fall into disappointment, when we do not see our goals fulfilled: those purposes on which we have put so much dedication on many occasions.

When we do not reach the culmination of that objective, of that which we have most longed for, an enormous disappointment comes over us, our self-confidence weakens and we begin to feel the oppression of those who feel overwhelmed by disappointment and anguish.

Surely, this makes us change direction, looking for other paths where we can find luck. In reality, our journey through life is like this: not always the route is the most appropriate, the one we desire; therefore we always have the option of looking for other paths along which to continue our journey.

In any case, it will always be a mistake to stop and consider the journey finished, not to look for other, more pleasant routes that are more in line with what we truly desire.

Taking advantage of what you have learned

In such a situation, you try to conduct yourself as best you can, trying to transfer all that you have learned -from your journeys that led you nowhere- to a new route, to a new way of walking along a path that at least makes you move forward, where you can feel a light that turns you on or something that sets you on fire inside and does not go out until you start acting again; to behave as if nothing had happened, without living in the disappointment that caused you that failure; far from the fatalism and sadness that sometimes causes the misfortune of not being able to live with optimism, when the joy of hope is lost and there is no longer any belief that there are other safer ideas to achieve the illusion of a new dream.

Not always what should be our eagerness is strong enough to act with the perseverance that is required. In many cases it is just a matter of maintaining a constancy -without the need to be too obstinate- that keeps our interest and the necessary attitude alive.

Sometimes, things come out not by talent, but by the capacity to maintain one's own will always with the same predisposition, giving preference to what we long for. He who is infatuated with always insisting on what he desires, normally has more possibilities of reaching it, his way of stubbornness brings him closer to the objective; in many cases, it is the only way to achieve what we aspire, there is no other formula.

TO RESORT TO CALM

They are moments in which it is also advisable to look for the calm, because thanks to this we can face those torments that only appear when the bitterness and the pain take possession of us and we do not know how to free ourselves of that load of pessimism.

Only if we establish a pause to value everything that is happening, as a whole, we can face the failure and disillusionment that accompanies all those disappointments that we often suffer when we see that our goals are not met, when we feel that destiny is still an ideal that we have not yet reached.

In those moments we need to stop to open a parenthesis, to seek in that interval an escape, an exit door that leads us to another place that makes us see things from another point of view, with another mentality and a new attitude more serene and away from that feeling of failure in which we are often trapped.

If we let ourselves be dragged by our own mind in such situations, we will surely insist, repeatedly, in that approach of frustration and disappointment; there are those who live permanently there and never get out.

Only if we are aware that we can intervene in this kind of processes, we will have the key to change the orientation, the sense of our judgments and the way we use our own reasoning.

Only if we act from reflection, we will reach the true knowledge, to achieve the necessary awareness to be able to promote a change that makes us rectify, innovate, transform our old purposes for new desires, new projects that awaken our interest and help us find a new purpose, a new destiny.

In such situations it is necessary to always look for calm: that peace that fixes our own understanding and brings everything back together, that lessens the conflict and restores our balance.

With it you will be able to give light to the conscience, to resolve in this way all those contradictions to which you feel subjected and that you have been turning little by little into problems, that you have been accepting without further ado because of your own inability to overcome them, to find a solution to all those confusions that move in your mind occupying all the space, eliminating all that clarity that you need to wake up, to exist in a much more conscious way.

When you attend to what is inside you, from the calm, you can distinguish all that stream of thoughts that are gradually being incorporated into your mind and that are absorbing your attention without you being very aware.

To get away from them and to be able to banish them, you only have to try to observe briefly all those thoughts that were hidden before and that in those moments extend deceiving the reality and falsifying the truth of everything that is exposed before you.

Only by using calmness can we aspire to probe that other murky part of our mind that deceives us and leads us along paths that alter who we are, that make us float in an imaginary world that leads us to live in fiction.

If you have the opportunity to contemplate all this, you will see the inaccuracy of many of your reasonings, the errors that are projected in your judgments, in the design of your beliefs, which are defined with each assessment you make of what is happening to you.

You can clearly distinguish all this, follow its development, if you go into a somewhat deeper level, through those intervals of silence that sometimes arise in the midst of all the mental agitation to which we are relentlessly subjected.

Everything becomes more visible in this way; everything that occupies your mind becomes more moldable in this phase. You can get to the origin of everything that manifests.

From calmness you can observe everything in a more impartial way, without being subjected to everything that comes from your own mind: all those components that intervene in your own thought that pile up until they manage to draw a world through which you try to escape at the slightest opportunity.

If you dominate that place and become master of your own consciousness, you will have won the most important battle, you will be above that which causes you suffering, since you will observe everything as a witness, distanced from your own mental content, as a mere observer who establishes a separation between himself and that which he observes: those contents and thoughts that come to your consciousness that are nothing more than illusions and material from the past.

If we do not learn to pause and stop in order to channel our own thinking, we will not distinguish reality from fiction; we will automatically immerse ourselves in a world of affirmations more typical of the imagination than of the real world.

If you abandon yourself only to what your mind proposes at all times, you will live in a loop that will lead you to an artificial existence: dependent on your habits, immobilized by your own thoughts, which will govern you as long as you continue to live in an unconscious life, barely appreciating everything that surrounds you in another, much deeper way.

Thanks to this means that is your own calm, you can suspend this irrational mechanism in which some thoughts are exalted by repeating themselves over and over again through vigorous impulses that are reproduced infinitely over time.

14. Influence

The world that surrounds us exerts an enormous power of permanent attraction on us, on our own will, in such a way that all our perceptive senses are only pending of everything that happens around us, which captivates us in such a way that makes us constantly paying attention to any stimulus that arises at all times.

We act immersed in a process that gives you a limited opportunity to be yourself. Normally we let ourselves be carried away by circumstances, without having the space to see things in a different way, from a more propitious terrain to calibrate the consequences with more rest; to act from tranquility and observe everything from a peace that keeps us away from anguish.

If this were the case, we would go through life with more confidence; many things would cease to affect us, because we would have a favorable mechanism to not be influenced by all those assumptions that invade us and that make us not appreciate that truth that always appears hidden but that we know is there, in every detail, hidden behind every appearance, as if it were a secret that can only be observed when the din of our own mind ceases.

We function in phases. Sometimes, depending on the circumstances and the type of previous experiences we have had, we can find ourselves euphoric, more motivated than usual; and at other times the opposite can happen: we can become more depressed, with less strength, with less energy to face the chores of our daily life.

We do not always maintain the same line in terms of what our mood may be, because it is affected by every little detail that happens in our lives: in what we observe; in everything that happens in our relationships with the people who surround us regularly...

Everything influences and affects us, so that our path, our future, does not always follow the same line. There are moments in which we deviate from the path, because of everything that happens around us and also inside ourselves, since sometimes mental contents arise, in the form of thoughts and images, which lead us along a certain path and end up affecting our own emotions - what we feel at each moment - and also influence the type of actions we end up performing; since if they are contents that are repeated more intensely, in the end, almost without us realizing it, we end up performing an action related to such contents.

All this makes that our life, sometimes, does not follow the line it should follow, that it has ups and downs and deviations due to all this: to the influence that the mind exerts on us and also to the influence of the external circumstances that surround us, which also affect us, since we cannot cease to exist in that environment in which we move daily, in which we develop our lives.

HOW TO COPE WITH INFLUENCES

If we were not to be affected by everything around us, we would have to live in isolation, but we are not made for that. We are social beings and feel the need to relate to others and to live in a concrete context in which we can develop both personally and socially, in the company of others.

Therefore, it is inevitable that all those things that happen around us, affect us, have consequences for us, both externally and internally.

Awareness and observation

This is unavoidable, but it is in our hands the way to deal with all those influences that come to us from outside; so that, if we are aware, all those external elements that affect us, stop exerting their power over us, because through awareness and slow observation we can divert everything that can influence us: all that we see outside of us.

Only by being conscious, we will observe in detail what happens within our own interior; we will not allow ourselves to be dragged by any influence, and much less by the din of unconscious thoughts that arise from the depths of our memory creating disorder and confusion that leads us to disorder: to the alteration of that peace that is hidden within, that is apart from the flows of the mind, beyond the constant traffic of images and ideas that run through our brain circuits.

When you are conscious you observe all that exists within you, you can free yourself from everything that has influenced you from the outside, that makes you experience an imbalance and turns you into someone different.

You will not be so easily influenced by all those distractions that often take hold of you and make you lose control, sometimes for too long.

You will abandon the dream of external reality; you will stop feeling the need to follow the stimuli that usually trap you, managing to influence your own behavior; you will begin to dominate every idea that comes to your consciousness, forgetting about time and all those matters that occupy you daily.

Thanks to observation we can achieve a separation between what we observe and ourselves, so that we can manage not to identify ourselves with those things that come from the outside, nor with all those contents that come from our inner world.

Sometimes, it is not so simple: to establish that barrier, that distancing by which we manage that nothing affects us, since our own human condition will always lead us to allow ourselves to be led by the power and influence exerted by the stimuli around us, and also by the impulses that are born from our own interior, which sometimes arise in an uncontrolled way, without us being very conscious of them.

He who manages to distance himself from all external influences will always find the best way to become himself at all times, in all circumstances. He will be able to achieve understanding and reach that wisdom that only those who discover themselves, who have reached the understanding of what they are, the knowledge of their "true essence", their authentic self, which has nothing to do with that other false self that is the ego, created through the identification with thought and that in most cases takes over us, forcing us to behave differently from what we really are.

Inner calm

To cope with all this process, it is necessary to get in touch with a situation in which you have control and mastery over this mechanism, and that can only be achieved through inner calm, in a situation away from external stimuli, which can distract you very easily and divert you from that path of inner peace that will always be beneficial for you, since it makes you meet yourself in a space within your own interior, away from unconscious and repetitive thinking.

15. Reality

The fact of reaching an explanation about what we are trying to find out does not mean that we can completely decipher all the intricacies that make up that reality. We only limit ourselves to intuit, to give our opinion about what we believe it is, based on what our understanding allows us to deduce from what we see.

In most cases, surely, there are many other elements that remain in the air, which are also important components and pieces of that factor, of that matter that we are trying to unravel.

Therefore, our understanding of reality only covers a small portion, that which we are able to discern thanks to the knowledge we already possess, the result of our past experiences.

That other part of reality that we are unable to interpret, because our knowledge has not yet achieved sufficient instruction, we leave for later, for when our reason discovers sufficient foundations to find a logical explanation for what we do not yet understand.

We can only appropriate reality if we master its most important properties, so it is always necessary to dwell on each and every one of its characteristics, not overlooking those elements that sometimes appear apart but are also necessary, because they are an integral part and pieces of that same reality.

Your own vision

In your analysis of the world you try to find an explanation looking for the causes of everything that happens. You look for contents and representations that are already in your memory, that are the product of past experiences, to try to formulate, in this way, a reflection that coincides with what you are observing; thus you arrive at your own vision of reality.

One thing is what you have in front of you at a given moment; and another is what you perceive, which may sometimes be similar, but other times may not be exactly the same.

And the fact is that everyone experiences reality differently, even if what is being observed is the same.

We appropriate each object we observe, in such a way that we end up incorporating it into our particular store of knowledge, but with very particular characteristics: those that we have subjectively placed on it, through our own interpretation.

In general, we are inclined to see things only from our point of view. In our own expressions it can be clearly seen that we use words in such a way that we always tend to modify the facts in order to tell our own version.

We use any gimmick to bring a conversation to our ground, to try to convince other people with our reasoning and our own vision of reality.

All the information coming from outside starts to coexist with all the knowledge we have previously acquired, so that in the end we create a rather subjective opinion of what we see. We can never be sure that we are in possession of the truth, because there is a patent process within us that distances us from the objectivity of things.

Even our own judgments are full of resolutions that we ourselves have created in our own minds. They are sentences with which we try to define and qualify what we see, but in reality they are nothing more than descriptions that have been formed in our conscience, that we make to expand our own understanding of the world, of everything that surrounds us; but they are still elaborations that we have made in our own mind, in a meticulous way, through terms that we already possessed, conclusions that we have been inventing over time to try to find an order in what surrounds us.

Through concepts and personal opinions, we shape our own vision of reality. We arrive at principles that help us create our own theories about life and ourselves.

Sometimes, these theories become a bit daring, because with time and experience we find that they are inappropriate, because they are based on beliefs that are closer to fiction than to reality itself.

The more factors you take into account when constituting your point of view, the easier it is to access that essential dimension of the truth of things; your degree of understanding will expand, reaching a magnitude that will allow you to always dwell on what really matters, on the transcendence and essence of what you see.

Everything will have a different meaning for you, because it will acquire a greater value and the appropriate level of importance, according to the usefulness that each thing has.

According to this way of proceeding, your interest will be adapted to a better use of everything that makes you improve as a human being, since this will reinforce your development and improve your growth, by raising your level of increasing attention only in those things that make you progress.

Reality is not what you imagine

At times, you allow yourself to be fascinated by the amazing power of your mind, which impresses you with its formidable and enormous wave of fantastic thoughts about the world around you; about the amazing things you could do and what you could achieve if you are more or less normal and behave like everyone else.

Until you suffer a reality check, when you see that what is around you is not what you had imagined, you see with your own eyes that what you find out there is not what you had experienced inside yourself, in the records of your own thinking.

You do not know the reason why this happens, but you witness, a little frustrated, a reality that suddenly occurs that you had not experienced before. Then you witness a present that you have to face away from your own thought, whose ideas are still running with a reasoning that is distant from what you are seeing before you.

So you understand that you need to make a logical and slow reflection, to analyze and explore more carefully what is happening and that you had not appreciated until that moment; that you had not taken into account, since your attention was lost deliberating on other considerations that had nothing to do with the reality in front of you.

We would all like to give a sense to all those issues that we do not know, but there are issues whose subject matter may not be in the scope of our understanding, because there will always be questions to be solved and many problems that we do not know how to face; because they are obstacles that exceed us, perhaps due to lack of knowledge or lack of experience on some occasions.

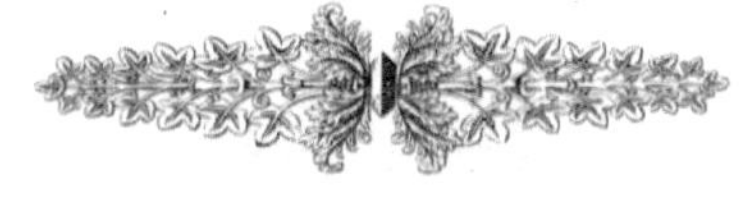

16. Time

Everything that exists in your memory can come to the light of your consciousness, spread throughout your mind without a definite order. Everything that is imprinted in your memories can become conscious again, through an impulse that raises it causing it to surface.

All the traces of your memory can become visible, recovering all those experiences that you once lived. In your mind can emerge all that is buried, all those elements that one day you repressed for some reason, until they occasionally come to light again and, with the help of your own understanding, manifest themselves again in your mind, reviving those emotions that you felt when they first appeared.

In reality, all the thoughts that your mind produces are elaborated through contents that you have been storing throughout the time, they are tied to everything that you have experienced previously, that returns to expose itself in your mind whenever you need to connect with any previous content to try to understand some aspect that appears in the present and that you find it difficult to distinguish.

Sometimes, the mind is an abyss in time that makes you escape from yourself and uses your past to plant seeds in the future.

This process, sometimes, you cannot control it, because it is loaded in you as a program with the purpose of moving your thoughts from one side to another; a program that in the end deceives you, because it makes you a slave of time and keeps you out of reality, without being conscious, without being able to think for yourself and lead your thoughts to the door where your "true self" is, where all the meanings and the root of "what you are" are.

If you follow your mind it is easy to be invaded by anxiety, because it is only guided by time, it needs time, to make you live in the past or pending the future; in such a way that you are always somewhere else and not there where your Being is; in that other deeper and absolute level where you meet yourself in a space where there is no past or future, where you feel you are alive and present in another new reality: a reality where there are no affirmations or noises; where you feel free of any control that your unconscious mind can exert on you.

Drawing on the past

Sometimes, we evoke thoughts with the idea of remembering the past, when we believe that today does not satisfy us, does not fulfill us. We resort to events far away in time, that already happened and that turned out to be satisfactory for us. We do it to find a reward, an excuse to repair the suffering we may be experiencing in the present moment.

We recreate ourselves in past experiences, especially in that which was to our liking, which happened just as we planned, with the idea of evading a reality that does not satisfy us, that in many occasions we encounter daily and that is full of a series of difficulties that we do not know how to solve.

That is why we go back in time, to place ourselves in those moments in which we were able to overcome the obstacles and be above the inconveniences; there are many people living in the past just for this reason.

It can happen that one is trapped in a series of circumstances in such a way that he/she is not able to clarify himself/herself to solve the problems, to make the best possible decision according to each situation.

There are periods in which one can feel a bit more burdened, more closed in on oneself and with less passion for things. Sometimes, we do not have enough fervor to remedy everything that oppresses us: all those details that cause anguish and provoke in us a constant worry that undoes us and overwhelms us.

Resorting to the past is a maneuver to escape from the present, to disappear for a while from those states of anguish that sometimes overwhelm us and do not allow us to feel that peace that can only be acquired when there is no concern, when calmness encompasses everything and life is a gentle and peaceful journey.

Before avoiding the present moment, because we do not like it, we should resort to calm, to face, in a more lasting way, all those negative emotions that we sometimes feel when we are overcome by a disenchantment that leads us to pessimism, to an anguish that brings us down in sadness, because we come to believe that we live in a complicated reality that holds us back and prevents us from achieving the joy and pleasure of happiness.

The future is only in your thoughts; it arises every time your mind wants to take you beyond the present, when it is not attractive enough or when you want to travel in time to abandon yourself in other moments that are yet to come.

Observing from the calm

If you stop, in silence, you will be able to connect with all that you once were, with all those experiences that now remain hidden in your memory but that one day taught you to appreciate the joy of life, or to feel the anguish caused by some difficulty.

You will be able to distinguish all these contents - which belong to your memories- very easily, if you observe from the calm all those elements that at a certain moment arise from your memory and that already appeared in the past.

If you witness all this happening in your mind, you will not waste your time on your own past, nor will you use the future as a means of evasion. You will perceive reality as it is, for you will not allow yourself to be led by that mechanical habit that leads you to concentrate your energies on a past that has already occurred, and on a future that is yet to come.

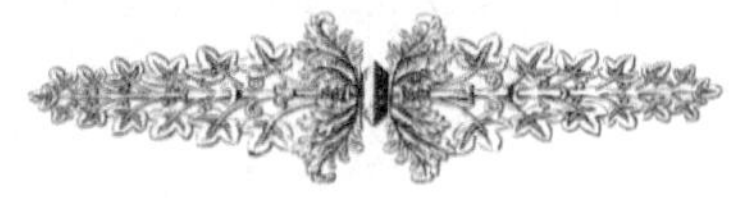

17. Understanding

Our judgments are filled with reasoning, evidence and conclusions that help us to register an explanation to each of the plots of what we observe, when sometimes we do not find the reasons: the raison d'être of those questions that still do not have a solution that convinces us.

Thanks to these considerations, our reason is being formed, we feel that our understanding has more sanity, that in our mind there are more opinions, and that the process of our own intelligence has more sense; a greater understanding of the origin of things, which is the source where the reasons are born, the reasons that make us have a purpose, that everything has a cause, even those issues that have no foundation, no foundation on which to rest.

All that is in our consciousness, in each moment, are loose components that emerge from our memory and form our knowledge when they are united with each other.

When we try to look for a reason or to understand that which we do not understand, what we do is to penetrate into those contents that we already have in order to look for related information that explains the matter we are trying to discern.

In reality, we look for arguments to elaborate our own judgments, to demonstrate with evidence our peculiar reasoning about what we are trying to know.

To do this, we use information that is already contained in our database, that has already been captured through experience, in our contact with the world around us.

What we do next is to relate those components that have a relationship, to find in this way a foundation, some principles that make us understand the origin of what we are trying to guess.

We can carry out this process thanks to all that previous knowledge that is stored in our memory, the result of the contact we have had with the world; of the type of communication established with those with whom we have related; of the information acquired through learning and the practice of our own behaviors, of the result of all our actions, through which we have acquired sufficient skills to be experts in certain matters.

Time

When we try to decipher that which we do not know, at first we are guided by a mere intuition that is barely enough to reach a complete knowledge of that which we are deducing. If we continue to take in information, in the end we obtain more complete, more conclusive and objective results; it all depends on the time we devote to researching what we have in front of us.

Curiosity

We only investigate things that make us curious for some reason: because of their uniqueness; because of their rarity or because they are significant to us for any other reason.

The fact is, we are not always driven to increase our own knowledge. We only want to attain the wisdom of what we understand to be important, relevant in some way, representative of the person we want to be.

If we are aware

You will get to understand everything when your tension decreases and your consciousness is free from the bonds of the mind. You will see that you have been in a dream world that has made you live in an invented existence, which constantly makes you go back to the past through thought, thus entering a kind of loop that conditions everything you plan to do in the future.

If we are aware of our own internal processes, we can reach the understanding and knowledge of our inner space.

To reach this degree of knowledge, an attitude of inward observation is required. It has to be done constantly, since in practice lies the secret of this way of knowing ourselves by accessing our inner world.

We will reach a wisdom about what we are that will make us better, because with this new information we will cover a wider field as far as the knowledge of our own reality is concerned. Knowing how we are, we will

understand ourselves, we will be closer to the truth of
the things that surround us.

Self-knowledge

When you know yourself you come to understand
all that you have not understood up to that moment.
Somehow you forgive yourself for the mistakes made
in the past; you find that everything has a logical and
reasonable explanation, that everything has a cause and
a reason for being, a background and an explanation.

You understand that for some things to have happened, others have had to happen, that the necessary
conditions have been previously established for a certain situation to appear to the detriment of another;
and that in most cases the living conditions in which
you live have actually been created by you, through
your behavior and your habits.

You come to realize that everything is in you, even
that which at that moment you are unaware of; that
many of the difficulties we go through are of our own
making; that we can stop our own mental rumination,
the repetitive thoughts, if we become aware of all that
goes on in our mind through observation and the establishment of a pause in moments of stillness and silence.

Self-knowledge gives you all these advantages, this
wisdom about life and about yourself that you did not
know before.

This clairvoyance only comes when one comes to
know oneself. In those moments everything has a new
meaning, both the things you do in life and the things
you stop doing; everything has a meaning.

You will soon see that the encounter with yourself is the best way to observe the world with a clean, clear and objective look, much closer to the truth of things, that this knowledge is the one that allows you to always walk in the right direction: the path from which you should never deviate.

We will see perfectly the origin of everything we did not know or did not understand. Many things will cease to be unknown to us, because from this knowledge we can come to understand them without the need for someone to explain them to us, without having to do more research in search of information to help us understand them.

Your degree of understanding of everything that happens will be greater and greater, because you will have the opportunity to pay more attention to every little detail of what appears in your consciousness, which is the vehicle of every content that is imprinted in your memory.

When you come to understand yourself, you understand many things that happen to you that previously had no explanation; or perhaps you had not had enough time to find one. Then it becomes much easier to guide you through life, because this self-knowledge is something like a tool that allows you to choose more reliably what is best for you at all times.

Through self-knowledge, you can understand your reactions to all those circumstances that have surrounded you, to the events that have happened to you (the experiences you have had to undergo, many of them traumatic).

The one who tries to understand himself, not only limits himself to the passing of the years, to what his experience can bring him, he tries to look inside himself to know more about himself, to understand the reality of the things that surround him and also to know everything that is inside himself, which leads him to behave the way he does.

Anyone who knows how to distance himself from the material world, who knows how to choose at each moment what is most convenient for him in all aspects, will always have an advantage over the rest, since he will have more information about himself and will reach a greater understanding of what he is and of the meaning of all those apparently incomprehensible things that surround us and that affect us so much without our realizing it.

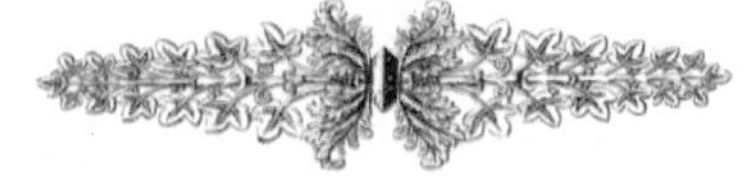

18. Purpose

To live a life with purpose is to have a series of objectives, a plan, to put all the effort that is possible with the intention of aspiring to fulfill them.

Whenever there is a desire, there is a determination, an idea of always looking in the same direction. Then there is the will with which we decide to approach that end, that goal.

Everyone has their own motives: the causes that are at the base and explain the behaviors and lifestyle of each one of us. You will see it clearly in the way of proceeding of all those who surround you, in how they act and conduct themselves through life.

In their behavior and attitude you will see, without effort, their objectives, the purpose that moves them when making their decisions; where they get the courage and audacity to face all those obstacles that are interposed, inevitably, along the way.

In many occasions our actions do not adjust to our true purpose, to that ultimate objective that we all have and that is determined by our deepest desires, by that final goal that we all have where we have deposited our illusion and hope.

At certain times we live in a delirium where we turn reality into a carousel of imaginary ideas that lead us to deception; to face a world where we live limited, without a purpose that fits what we really are, that defines us, that incites us to penetrate into the deepest part of ourselves to delve into "what we really are".

Thousands of ideas come to your head with the intention of fulfilling a certain purpose, your will depends on reaching that goal, although it requires a perseverance that makes you persevere firmly to achieve that goal, or that desire that you intend to fulfill.

In many occasions it can be that we do not have a concrete purpose, a desire or a project that captures our interest and that makes us feel useful, if with it we gain something in some sense, if we obtain some benefit.

In these cases, we find ourselves without a plan, we can get to do things without a pretense, without any will to reach a certain end.

It is possible that, sometimes, you do not have an idea, a reason to put all your efforts and your spirit. When this happens, it is necessary to insist with tenacity in looking for a destiny, a purpose to which to direct your actions; it will be the only way in which your life will have a value, if your existence and all your actions contain the force of a goal, of an illusion.

Only if we move away from thought, we establish a distance between our mind and what we truly are, which is beyond any mental content. In such a case we can find ourselves; establish contact with our "true essence"; discover the purpose that we all have within us, but that we rarely discover, since we are not used to getting in touch with that inner world to discover what we truly are.

It is the only way to find our "true purpose": that goal where we must lead our existence that leads us to act wisely, according to "what we are", to the true path that we must travel to lead a life with an intention.

It will shape your destiny

The kind of goals you set for yourself will form your destiny, which will shape you according to each of the actions you take, through all the daily activities you carry out. Your own enthusiasm and strength will be increased when, behind every act you perform, you verify that your purpose is materializing in easily observable results.

In this way, you will continue to be interested in that purpose, you will not abandon your intention to pursue that idea, nor the determination to achieve it through your eagerness and perseverance. You will find that leading a life with a pretense or an aspiration keeps you diligent, light, that all your power is based on the firmness of an ideal, of a purpose, which leads you to have a reason to live.

When someone is only focused on his intention, his interest and his eagerness always go hand in hand, with the sole purpose of reaching the goal. In those moments his ideal, his purpose, is his destiny, because he only applies himself to perform those tasks that lead him to the desired success.

When he reaches the achievement of what he had proposed, he understands that his project was worth-

while, that despite the difficulties it could be achieved.
He does not feel any kind of frustration, because his
expectations are fulfilled.

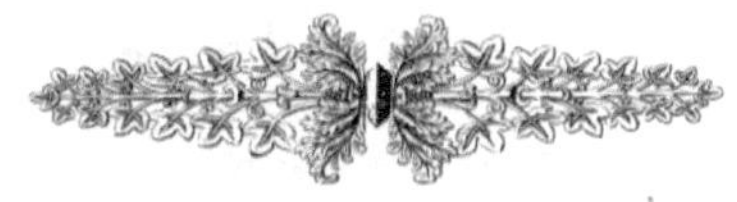

19. Hope

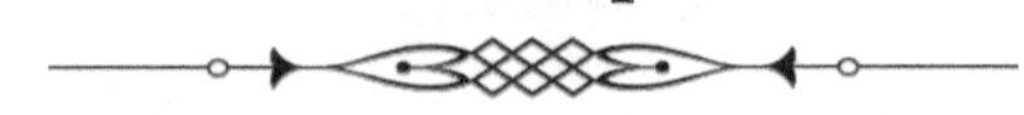

Our reason is nourished by opinions, convictions and other considerations that become judgments, ideas and beliefs that fill us with convictions for a certain period of time.

This leads us to have a certain security about what we think about the world, about the people around us and about everything that happens to us daily, in the course of our daily life.

We always need to believe in something, to have a certain evidence, to have the certainty that some things will happen in our life if we act in a certain way. This hope is necessary, because it fills us with confidence and allows us to have a clear illusion in the future, in what we aspire to achieve.

So everything we do we project it towards what we intend, feeding an illusion that becomes our ideal, something we imagine will happen if everything goes as we have planned.

Sometimes this longing is fulfilled, but on other occasions it remains a mere mirage, a simple chimera that we have invented to have, at least, an aspiration, a goal that keeps us alive the desire to continue to exist, to survive, even if there are many difficulties and impediments that we have to face.

Hope becomes, in this way, one of the main reasons to continue existing, to harbor a perspective that gives us a certain tranquility, although everything involves a risk and there is always the danger of fatality: of that misfortune that one feels when one has not been lucky, when a halo of misfortune invades us causing sadness and affliction.

Courage

That which we call courage, which is nothing more than that energy that comes from within ourselves and makes us dare to perform a particular action, is something that comes from our inner strength.

It is the fuel we need every day to face our daily life with enough strength not to fall down at the first change.

It is what keeps us going, in those moments of greatest weakness when our strength is compromised, when our endurance needs the help of our own will to continue acting with courage and with enough boldness to live with determination.

It is what gives us that strength that is determined by "the power of the intention", when we have interest in some matter that requires perseverance and all the effort on our part to fight with eagerness for that objective to which we aspire or for that passion that always occupies us.

Our spirit has to do with the yearning, with the eagerness that we put in what we pretend. It is the ardor, the impetus that leads us to the daily effort in those small tasks through which we gradually conquer our own destiny; our function, the task that allows us to have at least a direction, an occupation in which to remain active, where to consecrate that energy that is born from within ourselves to offer it to the world, through our dedication in our daily chores.

If we do not have courage, if we do not have any kind of resolution and courage, we will never be able to make the necessary decisions to continue progressing, to be able to manage conveniently in all those obstacles that in many occasions life presents us in the form of conflicts to which we have to find a way out; so that the end is always a good outcome for us, something that satisfies us, that relieves us from the pain of those falls that sometimes plunge us into a terrible frustration and make us shipwrecked in the decline, in a decadence that collapses us without discouragement, making us see the sunset and our own weakness.

Our courage is the best medicine against despondency, against that decay that we sometimes suffer when we do things without passion, without love, without the respect due to ourselves.

Inner calm

For those who have not yet found a way out, it may be advisable to look for those favorable moments to find stillness: that calm that leads us to observe everything with a peaceful, serene slowness, where we can find a new landscape, a new perspective that changes our focus and makes us find a new expectation, a way out of disappointment and all that frustration we feel when we do not reach the end, when we do not see the culmination of our ambitions, when our goal remains a mere purpose, an unresolved end.

Only from that place we can see everything from another position, from a location that makes us see things in a much more impartial, more objective way.

Your mind will always remind you of all those illusions that you need to keep feeling alive, to maintain hope and thus be able to reach certain levels of optimism that allow you to cope with the day to day, even if sometimes you are invaded by confusion and you do not find the means to release it.

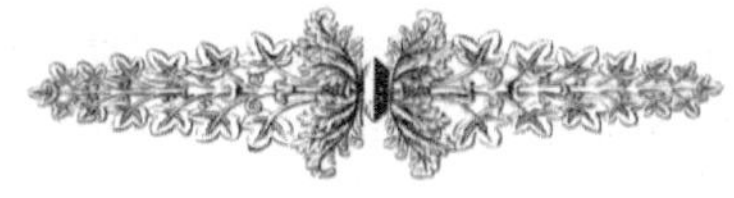

ABOUT THE AUTHOR

Manuel Triguero has a degree in Psychology from the Pontifical University of Salamanca (Spain). As a counselor he has had the opportunity to help a great number of people individually.

In his books he shares his experience in the field of human development, trying to capture his reflections and all those discoveries that can become tools to help self-knowledge and personal transformation.

They are an invitation to all those people interested in this kind of content to investigate their own inner self, to awaken their capacity to know themselves and to live in the best possible way.

www.ingramcontent.com/pod-product-compliance
Lightning Source LLC
LaVergne TN
LVHW092355170726
843489LV00001B/196